MY
HENKELINDA

MY
HENKELINDA

Nancy Philippi

Library of Congress Control Number:		2014912716
ISBN:	Hardcover	978-1-4990-5169-8
	Softcover	978-1-4990-5170-4
	eBook	978-1-4990-5168-1

This book was printed in the United States of America.

Rev. date: 07/25/2014

To order additional copies of this book, contact:
Xlibris LLC
1-888-795-4274
www.Xlibris.com
Orders@Xlibris.com
602883

To Hatixhe and Henkelinda, with my greatest admiration

CONTENTS

Chapter 1

MY WORLD

Mary and I took the tram from Sarajevo, Sunday morning, and although new street cars had been donated by the Japanese government after the war, the recently repaired tracks made for a slow and bumpy ride. Our plans were vague, our spirits high and our stomachs queasy in anticipation of what we were about to do. At the end of the line, in the shattered town of Ilidza, where so much of the fighting had taken place, a line of taxis manned by sleeping drivers stretched out into the silent, shabby plaza.

"Shall we?" I nodded toward the cabs.

"How else will we find it?"

"The Kosovo refugee camp in Hadžići," I enunciated carefully to the driver in English.

"Da, Coca Cola," he said.

We were okay. Colleen, an American expatriate helping the Bosnians rebuild their country, had told us the refugees were housed in the old soft drink factory.

Colleen was to have been our guide but over a gritty Bosnian coffee, an hour earlier, she had backed out.

"Why!" Mary demanded.

"I don't want to overload my soul."

Colleen took herself too seriously for our taste – an error in our judgment, not hers.

No one that we knew in Sarajevo had visited the camp, perhaps for the same reason in this badly wounded city that had already made such demands on souls.

"Maybe we shouldn't go either," I said, after Colleen left.

"We can always turn back," said Mary.

"Right," I answered. Mary never turned back.

Our taxi bumped along the narrow roads, past bombed out houses and piles of rubble. It pulled up at a complex of industrial buildings.

"Coca Cola," our driver grinned. I overpaid in Deutschmark – I never seemed to get it right – and we got out. He whipped a U-turn and sped off.

"Should we have asked him to wait?" I asked the air.

Mary was already striding toward a trailer outside the gate of a huge fenced-in compound that was presumably the United Nations refugee camp, although no signs proclaimed it so. I trotted after her and we climbed up into a dark, messy office, full of people who, with the exception of a woman on a telephone, had no apparent function.

"Yes?" the woman put her hand over the mouthpiece.

"We'd like to visit the camp."

"Go right ahead," she said curtly.

"Will people speak English?"

"Not likely. We have a translator but he is busy now and you'll have to wait," she replied and turned back to her conversation. We stepped back outside.

"Now what?"

I'd already lost my taste for this adventure, sensing that these people had no time – nor patience – for tourists like us.

"Let's just go in," said Mary, and she headed for the gate.

We walked through the opening in the ten foot chain link fence into another world. Hundreds of people milled about. Men lounged around the perimeter, most of them smoking, many watching us. Clusters of women stood talking among themselves and a few kerchiefed heads swiveled unsmiling in our direction. A line of squat grey tents stretched off to our right, and three long low characterless buildings loomed beyond. Smells from a nearby row of porta-potties wafted over. We voyeurs – that's how I saw us – had stepped from the world's mainstream into a backwater of truly overloaded souls. We had no business in this place.

"What are we doing here?" I muttered, "let's go!"

"Give it a minute," Mary answered.

The children came, a few at first, then more, until we were surrounded by a small crowd, from giggling toddlers to sullen teenagers.

"Do you speak English?" we asked, turning from one to another without getting words back that we recognized. I hated it. We two *Lady Bountifuls* from America had nothing to offer them but our own self-centered curiosity. Feelings of panic mixed with my shame and I wanted out, with or without Mary, who was busy doing a sign language thing with some ragtag little boys.

The noise level was rising, the faces blurred together and the swirling in my head verged on dizziness, as something cramped my gut – less fear than foolishness.

Someone touched my right arm.

"I speak English," said a husky female voice.

I turned to face the big brown eyes of a young woman, her head tilted slightly forward so that her scrutiny of me upward through thick lashes was almost coquettish. Everything about her shone – her smile, her skin, her hair – and she radiated intelligence and good spirits. I was enchanted.

"Who are you?"

"I am Henkelinda."

* * *

Two months earlier this girl, who had just entered my world so magically, would have had no place in it. I had stood on a New Hampshire hilltop overlooking the Connecticut River Valley, while behind me a shimmering wedding tent soared elegantly to the sky. As I sipped a white Bordeaux, waiting for the outdoor ceremony to begin, the mother of the bride dashed over for a quick hello. Mary had been my college roommate forty years before.

"I'm so glad you came, although I won't get much time to talk. Family responsibilities, you know."

"Tell me in two words, how is your life?" I asked.

"Wonderful," she said ". . . almost."

The "wonderful" I understood – the dream house built within a nearby copse of trees when her husband retired, her thriving practice as a psychotherapist, and children and grandchildren nearby.

"Why the 'almost'"?

"I just got a DUI," she said.

A thunderbolt out of the soft blue New England sky!

No rip-roaring roadhouse drunk, she'd polished off enough white wine during an art gallery reception to set off a breathe analyzer, and what I knew that the police in the darkened car just past the turnoff onto her mountain road didn't, was that she always took corners too fast. But the judge made no allowance for eccentric drivers and her license had been suspended for six months, making it logistically difficult and emotionally humiliating to work – small town newspapers make good sport of solid citizens who slip up. Those 180 days were passing at a ponderous pace.

"Why don't you get away – take the trip you've been talking about – to Bosnia," I suggested.

"I'm dying to go to Sarajevo," she said, "but not alone, and no one wants to come along."

"I'll go with you," I said. Just like that it popped out, the commitment I had never thought to make. Bosnia meant little to me.

The energy in the scudding clouds, the wine, some passing pixie – one or all had suddenly conspired to change my life.

"You will?" she gasped.

"When do we go?"

"October! she said, not being one to hem and haw.

"Let's do it," I replied, challenged, as always, to match her quick step pace.

A New Hampshire mountain-top wedding

The first squawks of a bagpipe reached our ears as, leading the long slow bridal procession from the house, a kilted musician stepped into distant view followed by a radiant Kathleen on the arm of her father, Dick. The mother of the bride dashed back to her aging aunts. Vows were exchanged and speeches made, mounds of lobsters and gallons of champagne consumed and I dragged most of the old fogies and several young ones onto the dance floor as the blues band played into the balmy August night. The next morning there was talk over a leisurely breakfast, goodbyes, and by dark I was back in Indiana, with plans to make and things to do.

Mary's main interest in Bosnia was in the children allegedly produced by the systematic raping of Bosnian women by Serbian soldiers and paramilitary. These unwanted babies, it had been rumored, were deprived of affection and isolated in orphanages. It was a natural thing for Mary to respond to global suffering. Her parents had been medical missionaries in mainland China, where she was raised, and she had later worked with them in a North African clinic. In her psychotherapy practice, she kept a foot in two worlds – one working pro bono with indigents in Vermont, the other among affluent customers in New Hampshire, and she always had more non-paying clients than the other kind.

We had first met at a boarding school founded by evangelist Dwight Lyman Moody on the banks of the Connecticut River as it passes through Massachusetts. She had just been hurried out of Mao's China, increasingly hostile to missionaries, and I had been more or less homeless since the violent death of the only father figure I'd ever known. That school nurtured our souls along with our minds. It was where I first rubbed shoulders with the *charity* to which Mary had been bred. After graduation we looked forward to lives of do-gooding and making-a-difference kinds of stuff.

After prep school Mary and I were roommates at a college further south in the same river valley, where she majored in religion and went on to nursing school while I eventually left for the Anthropology Department at the University of Chicago. And although we saw little of each other for many years, our lives followed similar paths, ones that took us far from where we started out. We discovered men and as our hormones took charge, Mary fell in love with an Italian preacher and I with a Mexican archaeologist. After finally disengaging from these fairy tale amours we both married clean-cut east coast MBA's with feet on the first rungs of their respective corporate ladders. Romantic love had shot down our more noble aspirations. It is, as John Updike says, "the fever by which Nature gets her work done," and *her work*, in each of our cases, was two girls and one boy. In the midst of this slippage into the mainstream our husbands' jobs had brought us to the same city, where we discovered a new compatibility. Only recently had our paths diverged again.

I had always deluded myself into thinking that marriage and child rearing were only a brief detour in my life's journey, as they deviously became the journey itself. For more than forty years my do-gooding had been of the convenient, conventional kind. When I reached out a hand to help, by giving money or volunteering time, I did it from the safety of deep inside my world. My core remained unscathed.

Scathing, however, sometimes occurred during the six o'clock TV news. It began with the Vietnam war, where I couldn't watch the images of suffering without vicarious pain. I cried, I raged, I anguished, along with those who had real reason to. The Balkans had been a more recent case in point. I'd agonized over the fate of the Croatians and Bosnians during the first half of the nineties, as images of massacres flashed across the screen, and I'd cursed first the United Nations and then my own government for not coming to their rescue, but those ersatz emotions had no reality in my life. Now I was going to Sarajevo, to be part of it and let it be part of me, and I dreaded the demands that it might make. I needed to prepare and so I went to the local library and in the two months before our trip, read through the Balkan collection.

First, I pulled out the histories to get the facts.

Six republics (Serbia, Croatia, Bosnia-Herzegovina, Macedonia, Slovenia and Montenegro) had been welded together to form Yugoslavia after the Second World War by Marshall Tito, the hero of guerilla resistance to the Nazis. This federation was populated largely by physically indistinguishable, ethnically identical "south Slavs" (*Yug* means *south* in Serbo-Croatian) who spoke the same language but, due to historical circumstance, practiced different religions, roughly associated with the three largest republics – Roman Catholicism in Croatia, Eastern Orthodox in Serbia and Islam in Bosnia-Herzegovina. After Tito's death in 1980, Ivan Stambolic became the Yugoslav president, followed by Slobodan Milosevic in 1987. Yugoslavia had always been ruled from the Serbian capitol on the Danube, Belgrade, and the majority Serbians had dominated the national economic and political life, producing resentment among the other ethnic groups. Under Milosevic this Serbian hegemony intensified. That much was history.

What happened next was the tumultuous events that I had followed haphazardly throughout the nineties. As the iron curtain collapsed across Eastern Europe, the non-Serbian states broke free of the Yugoslavian federation: Slovenia and Croatia declared independence in June of 1991, as did Macedonia that September, followed by Bosnia-Herzegovina in 1992. Each secession eroded Serbian power, not only by shrinking the realm and influence of President Milosevic but also by reducing the many Serbs scattered throughout the newly independent republics to a minority status in the new countries. Having so recently been the favored and sometimes overbearing majority, the Serbs' resentment at loss of privilege and fear of retribution was used by Milosevic to generate hostility and often violence against their neighbors, as he provided external military pressures of his own.

As the two most important states, Croatia and Bosnia, declared their independence, President Milosevic aimed the Yugoslav army – fourth largest in Europe – against the relatively unarmed seceding republics, with devastating results. Fierce attacks on Croatia designed to break the back of that newly independent country and suck large portions of it into a "greater Serbia," caused massive destruction and suffering in the fertile Croatian agricultural area known as the Krajina, particularly in the city of Vukovar, which fell to Serbia in November, 1991. Then Milosevic-backed Serbs attacked Sarajevo, the capitol of Bosnia, in the spring of 1992, and kept it under a deadly siege for almost four years, until a cease fire was forced in October, 1995, by NATO intervention.

A month later the major Balkan powers met under United States auspices and diplomat Richard Holbrook's persuasive leadership in Dayton, Ohio, where they put together a patchwork of ethnic sovereignties and ended the fighting, although it satisfied none of the parties. The Dayton Peace Accord was signed by Serbia, Croatia and Bosnia on November 21st.

One subject that some had hoped would be put on the Dayton agenda was a small Serbian province, Kosovo, where trouble had been brewing since the late 80's, when Milosevic had begun to systematically remove rights from the Albanian (Muslim) majority in favor of the Christian Orthodox Serb minority. His paramilitary forces there were commanded by some of the same leaders, practicing the same techniques of coercion, as had been used against the new republics. The gradual emergence of an armed Albanian resistance force portended future trouble, but the parties at Dayton were unwilling to dilute their own agendas by wrangling over Kosovar interests. In the late summer of 1998, as I pillaged the public library shelves and Bosnians struggled to implement their peace, those 1995 Kosovar rumblings were crescendoing to a roar.

These were the facts, as many once knew and far fewer remembered, including me. But it was the impassioned commentators who brought the major events and dates to life, writers who experienced or seen some part of it. I read Robert Kaplan's Balkan Ghosts, which concludes by grandiosely paraphrasing King John: *"Conflicting ethnic histories, inflamed by the living death of Communism, had made the Balkan sky so foul that now, sadly, a storm was required to clear it."* This author, who was among the earliest to blame the Yugoslavian wars on "ancient ethnic animosities" was suggesting that the bitter conflicts of the past – between the murderous Croatian *Ustache* who sided with the Nazis and our equally murderous allies, Serbian *Chetniks,* in World War II – made the Yugoslav war inevitable. It was rumored that this pompous little book had persuaded statesmen around the world, including our own president, not to interfere. They hate each other, always have and always will, went the argument, so let them simply fight it out – there's nothing we can do.

Harvest in the Snow, a little book by a Chicago woman, Ellen Blackman, had the biggest impact on me. It described the hellhole that Sarajevo became during those four long years of siege, for her and other western journalists who came under Serbian fire from the moment their arriving aircraft dove steeply down to the Sarajevo landing strip, through the weeks and months they were holed up in the city's Holiday Inn. The motel chain that symbolizes color coordinated mediocrity in the rest of the world became a focal point for western compassion for Bosnia's fate, providing a bunker whose rooms on the side exposed to Serbian gunners were uninhabitable, from which a desperate run through the parking lot could end in death. An ordinary Chicago woman, as I had recently been, her endurance of such trauma moved me enormously. Blackman described the deprivations and dangers that Sarajevo's residents suffered, dashing for cover from snipers as they left their homes for the little food that was available and denuding their parks of trees for fuel to survive the bitter winters; the sadism of the Serbian sharpshooters amassed on the hills that surrounded the little valley city; the 10,000 men women and children who died during that time. Turning the pages rapidly, I lived and breathed the horrors of those days.

The most painful reading was about the indifferent role the western powers played, passively watching as atrocities were documented by journalists who brought their stories out of Bosnia and Croatia – folks dragged from their homes, women raped, children beheaded, men of all ages lined up and machine gunned from behind – and refusing in the end to act. What hurt me most, perhaps, was the ineptitude of the United Nations. Boutros Boutros Galli, who recently had become Secretary General, had captured my imagination through his doppelganger in Lawrence Durrell's Alexandrian Quartet and I expected great things from the international organization under his leadership. Stories of the UN's role in Bosnia, as it concealed its impotence under an arrogant neutrality while vicious killings and naked aggression proceeded forward, disabused me of my positive expectations. Of all the grotesque stories, Srebrenica was the worst.

The subtitle of David Rohde's Endgame: the Betrayal and Fall of Srebrenica, Europe's Worst Massacre Since World War II, says it all. In early June of 1995, 25,000 Bosnian Muslims trapped in Srebrenica, a city that had a population of 8,000 before the siege, were starving, lacking medical aid, housing, water, food and electricity. After a long stand-off during which the Bosnians pleaded for international help, the heavily armed Serbian Army (VRS) overwhelmed the rag tag defending Bosnian militia and crashed into the town, guns blasting, driving helpless civilians from their homes. In the immediate aftermath the commanding Serb general, Ratko Mladić, marched the seven thousand Bosnian men who had been taken prisoners into the countryside, never to be seen again. Seven thousand, I repeated to myself out loud.

This story was ugly enough by itself but what made it intolerable to me was that Srebrenica had been designated as a "safe area," by the United Nations, who had sent a small Dutch peace keeping force to protect the city. Instead of providing protection, however, the out-manned Dutch soldiers quickly fell back to safety behind the town, letting the VRS overrun the UN posts on their way to total victory. All this was done as NATO planes circled minutes away, poised to deliver the missiles that would have insured that the UN "safe area" was truly safe. But those missiles were never sent as the airmen waited in vain for orders from the UN officials who dithered and double-talked in Zagreb and failed to issue the single order that would have saved those seven thousand men.

And while the performance of the small Dutch contingent, so mentally and militarily unprepared for the job of guaranteeing Srebrenica's safety, was no more shameful than that of the UN high command who had the means at hand to save them, and surely no more shameful than my own country's Secretary of State refusing to step in because "we have no dog in that fight," the Netherlands' Secretary of Defense outdid them all by actually asking the UN to refrain from air support for the Muslims because it might jeopardize the lives of his little cadre of uniformed countrymen. Thirty Dutch soldiers sent to protect 25,000 Bosnians and those thirty valued over and above the rest. It was not an easy book to read.

Among the ignominious events that occurred in Srebrenica was the moment when the Dutch Commander, Colonel Thom Karremans, was bullied into holding a champagne glass high to Mladić's for a photo op, after the routing had occurred and as one quarter of the population was being rounded up for execution. It wasn't champagne, protested Karremans, later, as if there was more honor in water than in wine. History is full of horror stories but this one occurred in *my* time and so I felt a share of the blame. While Srebrenica was being devastated, Dutch soldiers running for cover, and United Nations officials dithering in Zagreb, I had been building fences and planting tulip bulbs on my Indiana property, worlds away. This was not the only horror story of the 90's – an equally ghastly one had played out in Rwanda – but it was the one that I was going to have to personally confront. I was going to Sarajevo.

The guns had been still on the hills above Sarajevo for three years, the tanks were gone, and grass grew on the graves. And yet, because Slobodan Milosevic had so recently turned a new military fury against the nearby Serbian province of Kosovo, our families viewed our trip as dangerous and urged us not to go. One week before we left, Holbrooke went to Belgrade as a U.S. envoy, to demand that Milosevic stop the escalating persecution of the ethnic Albanians in Kosovo. His demand was delivered with a threat: if the Serbian army did not stop destroying Kosovar villages and murdering civilians, said Holbrooke, NATO would make it stop with military force. I didn't believe that threat. If we had done nothing to save the Sarajevans, who were these Kosovars to get more attention from either the United States or NATO? And even if the threat was well-intended – after all, NATO had eventually lost patience with the United Nations' diddling around and bombed the Serbs in Bosnia – Milosevic could easily come up with schemes to deflect bombing from an international community to whom bombing was anathema. I believed, as I was sure Milosevic did, that the west was far too lily-livered to get involved.

So I was surprised to get a call from Mary's husband, Dick. As good friends as we were, communication usually was conducted through his wife. He was angry, at both her and me.

"Don't you realize how dangerous the Balkans are?"

Danger is many things to many people and my perception was very different from Dick's. Sarajevo might not be a tourist paradise but it was a place where ordinary people were going about the business of rebuilding their lives. We might be in the way but, in my mind, we wouldn't be in danger.

"We've checked it out. I'm sure it's safe."

"It won't be if that Kosovo mess erupts."

"Mary and I will meet in Zurich and, if NATO decides to use military action, we'll change our plans," I said.

I lied. His wife and I had been exchanging daily e-mails, pumping each other up. Nothing could deter us from going on to Bosnia. My readings had wound me tighter than a top and the trip would provide relief to the angry guilt I felt. As for Mary, she had been lining up interviews with social agencies in Sarajevo and had an agenda a mile long.

"It's only the countryside, where there are still unexploded land mines, that is dangerous," I continued, disregarding – as Dick probably had as well – my lie.

"I'm not worried about the mines; I'm worried about those people. They're crazy over there, they'd take American hostages if the bombing starts and probably even if it doesn't. The world's a dangerous place, Nancy."

I was being talked down to and it freed me to get angry. Where did he get this notion of "over there," and "those people," and that all the world was mad – except for us, presumably! He thought with blinders on! Although Dick had spent a lot of time in Russia, doing business for his former corporate employer, he now saw the world beyond his mountaintop as a distasteful and frightening place. But I was fond of this charming and intelligent man and calmed down enough to take him seriously. I spelled out for him my thinking, that there were two ways we could be taken hostage – either by doing something unbelievably rash, under circumstances turned far uglier than they were now, or by that one in a million chance of being at the wrong place at the wrong time. The latter was as likely as being hit by lightning, as was the former if we behaved prudently. Prudence was not Mary's specialty but I assured Dick that it would be mine. To the extent that she took risks, and she often did, I'd be there to hold her back.

"Don't worry, we'll be fine," I told him.

"I have no reason at all to think that you'll be fine!"

I'd heard him angry before, but not at me. He was accustomed to getting his way, and wanted to convince me not to go, having failed with Mary. It hadn't worked.

"Just promise that you'll stay in touch with the American Embassy," he said.

I promised somberly, acceding to this glimmer of the hard edged power he had wielded all his working life. We hung up.

There was something worrying me far more than physical danger.

When I was ten and living on a New England farm with my widowed mother, her bachelor brother and their father, my uncle's foot slipped on the tractor's clutch and its two small front wheels rose high in the fresh blue Saturday morning sky and somersaulted backwards, crushing the life from the man I loved best in all the world. My grandfather discovered his crushed son gasping last breaths and raced back to the house, if an old man with a heart condition who hobbled about with a cane can be said to race.

"A chain," he shouted hoarsely into the empty air as he reached the farmhouse, "get a chain." I was the only one who heard, before he reached the phone, and off I went, into the dark depths of the horse barn, digging among rusty machinery parts and piles of junk next to the two gentle work horses who had been given this Saturday off, who never would have turned upon the man as had their mechanical replacement. I stumbled through the woodshed, the toolshed, the corn bin and even the chicken coop in fruitless search for the chain I believed would save my uncle's life – and mine. There was no one in that black universe that morning except me and my uncle, the man who read the comics to me every Sunday, taught me to read before I went to school, and although I could not see for the tears blinding my eyes, his life depended – of that I was dead sure – on my finding a chain. I ran and cried and cried and ran and scarcely noticed when the men and boys from other farms arrived with chains and trucks and more tractors, pushing me out of the way as they too failed to save my uncle but in a far more manly manner.

I retreated into the parlor – it was what we called that musty room we never used – and rocked back and forth sobbing until someone came to take me to my horseback riding lesson, attempting to impose normality on this worst day of my life, pretending and demanding that I pretend in return, that the sky was blue, not black. And later, overhearing the words "he's dead," spoken and then interpreted to me as "we're talking about a horse," I was further denied entrance to the world in which others dealt with this calamity in important adult ways, isolating me in my own misshapen one where it had been my job to save my uncle and I had failed. It was an unbearably lonely place to be.

And so I learned early the bleak outer limits of desperation combined with helplessness that have visited me off and on since then and when confronted with a crisis I am consumed by a crazed need to do, to solve, to save. It is the archetypal nightmare of my life, where, on the one hand I imagine myself to have the superwoman strength to save the day and, on the other, I am unable to do so. As I prepared to leave for Sarajevo, I had felt that bad dream close at hand, yet in my first encounter with Henkelinda, I did not recognize its harbinger.

CHAPTER 2

ZAGREB STOPOVER

Mary sat in the Zurich airport's departure lounge, angry. Not at me for being late, although I was, but at the paraphernalia at her feet. She carried a 30-pound braille typewriter, which had cost her great effort and $800, and stuffed into her shoulder bag was a pair of men's snow boots, size 10. Not her idea, either one, but the fruits of her generosity. Mary rarely refuses a favor but in return she feels entitled to her rage.

"It's so damned heavy," she said, shoving the typewriter to the side so I could settle beside her.

"Why are you doing this?" I asked, being better than her at saying no.

"It's braille, for god's sake, braille. For blind people who've been victims of a war. Get it?"

"And the boots?"

"Who knows? Maybe I'm saving his sister postage. But we're seeing their mother, so how could I refuse?"

I'd come from Chicago, she from Boston, to fly together to Zagreb and then on to Sarajevo.

"Is Dick okay about this trip?" I asked.

"Of course not. It drives him crazy that I've ignored his advice."

"Is that what it's about?"

"Of course."

"And not about you?"

"Hardly!"

Her tone suggested that I still didn't get it, after all these years. And I didn't, not all of it anyway. I knew her husband thought he understood the Balkans better than we did, which he didn't. He believed that the State Department's web-posted warnings should be the final say on where one should or shouldn't travel. But I wasn't so sure that he did not fear for the safety of his wife of 40 years. And I guessed that he would worry continually until she was home again, although his reasons probably had less to do with love than need. He couldn't live without her, I suspected, although he went to extremes to hide it from her. He told me once, after consuming eight ounces of gin, that he hated being alone in their house for even one night. This from a man who tolerated other people's company only with great effort – and usually only over cocktails. He didn't care for other people and he couldn't bear being totally by himself, a dilemma which she alone resolved. Of all the choices this wealthy successful man had made in life, his most important had been Mary. Being ashamed of this great need, he hid it behind bluster. That was my five-and-dime store analysis of their relationship. I had seen as deeply into it as any other third party, which nevertheless meant that I had seen very little. It's not easy for an outsider to penetrate the mysteries of intimate relationships and Mary's efforts to steer me in wrong directions may have been as manipulative as Dick's.

Our flight was called and I followed Mary and her baggage onto the bus, across the tarmac and up the metal steps. A strong wind whipped our scarves about our faces and I realized that we'd take off in a gusty crosswind, the plane would flip over and all the passengers would die. But while I was anticipating imminent death, as I usually do when boarding airplanes, Mary was trying to jam the typewriter under the seat.

As it turned out, we lived to land in Zagreb, where our excitement propelled us to burst through the one way doors into the arrival lounge without picking up our luggage, requiring an embarrassing backtrack through a bureaucratic maze, which deflated our good opinion of ourselves. Less important to Mary, who left life's luggage behind regularly, the gaffe suggested that I might be unqualified to act as Dick's surrogate.

Mary and I had had trouble with border bureaucracies once before, when a heavily-armed Jordanian soldier marched us back across the Jordan River to Israel because we did not have the proper papers, although we no longer had our Israeli visas, having surrendered them to Jordanian passport control. The Israeli soldiers who met us had a sense of humor, for no reason that I could comprehend, and after first scaring us to death, jokingly waived the bureaucratic nonsense and let us back into their fragile country.

We cabbed to Zagreb's Palace Hotel whose old world elegance I had once visited during cold war days: Queen Anne's curtains were draped seductively at the windows and courteous tuxedoed waiters believed, as Tito intended, that they owned the hotel. All that charm had been expunged by large panes of glass and modern efficiency at the reception desk. Venetian blinds were at the windows.

We hurried out into the street, afraid of succumbing too early to the exhaustion of our 30-hour day, and spent the late afternoon wandering about the main square, sipping at a gritty Croatian coffee as we watched begging gypsy women carrying bundles of rags to simulate babies and listened to a piping Bolivian musical group. We were the first customers in the hotel dining room at 7 PM and soon after went to bed.

It was the night of October 12th and at 2 A.M. European time, NATO Secretary General Janvier Solano announced that NATO had authorized air strikes on Kosovo, although not to occur for 96 hours. We saw the Solano press conference because, at midnight, our hotel room phone had rung. My bed was nearest so I picked it up. The voice that spoke was Dick's.

"You must go to the airport immediately," he said, "get out before it's too late."

What was the matter with this man!

"Too late for what?"

"They're going to attack Kosovo; there will be a rush to get out."

"Dick, we're in Croatia."

"I thought you were in Zagreb."

Where we were was ensconced in comfortable beds in a well-run hotel in an old and civilized city of a strong new country, but on Dick's map of the world we were only in a danger zone. I was too sleepy and irritated to bridge the gap.

"Hold on."

"It's for you." I passed the phone to the other bed and put my head under the pillow where I nevertheless strained to hear the muffled words.

"I told him we'd check with the United States Embassy in the morning," was all Mary said when she hung up 10 minutes later.

"Why did you tell him that?"

"Otherwise he'd never have left us alone."

"So, we'll do it."

"Right."

And then, "I also said that if they tell us not to go to Sarajevo, we'd go to Sicily."

"It's probably more dangerous there."

"Right."

The phone rang again.

"How're you doing, Nancy?" asked my son-in-law Mike.

This time I sat straight up, my nerves aflame.

"Is something wrong? Is Paula okay?"

"Everyone's fine. We just got a call from Dick. He told Paula to make you come home right away. She asked me to deal with it."

Damn Dick, anyway, scaring my kids! And poor Mike, being tossed this hot potato by my daughter, who had neatly side-stepped the request.

"Mike, believe me, everything's okay. Dick has some crazy idea that NATO is going to start bombing. Mary promised him we'd check with our embassy tomorrow, but things are just fine here – even the food."

Mike had less use for global politics than he did for food. He cooked to relax from his stressful job at the Chicago Options Exchange.

"Like what?"

"Meatballs for dinner – very spicy."

"That would have to be Cevapcici."

"Whatever. Thanks for calling. Goodnight."

"Goodnight? What time is it there?"

"Midnight."

We weren't on either Dick's map or Mike's clock. Instantaneous communication does not always make the world a smaller place.

Lying there wide awake, in what was late afternoon back at our homes, we turned on CNN, which was how we happened to catch the NATO Secretary General's press conference. What we'd learned about the Kosovar situation since we decided to go to Sarajevo provided us with good background for this turning point in Milosevic's relations with the western world.

Our own State Department and European governments had been watching, during 1998, as Serbian military and paramilitary forces moved through Kosovo, killing close to 2,000 Albanian Muslims and forcing almost half a million of them from their homes. Public opinion had been mobilized in support of the Albanians as rumors of two particularly barbarous incidents had filtered out from the western Kosovar region of Drenica early in the year. All the men in one family, the Ahmetis, had been murdered by Serbian militia in Likoshane in February and two months later an assault on the Jashari family compound near Srbica had killed 58 family members, including children and old men. While the United Nations had passed Resolution 1160 at the end of March, condemning the excessive use of force by Serbian security forces against Kosovar civilians and the US had called Richard Holbrooke back into service to negotiate with Milosevic, the Serbian leader quietly continued the ethnic cleansing at which he had proven himself so adept in Bosnia and Croatia. Reports of these two and other massacres prompted Solana to wisecrack off the record, during the following summer, that Milosevic's motto was "a village a day keeps NATO away." Finally, on September 23rd the United Nations passed a second, stronger resolution, Number 1199, that called for an immediate cease fire, withdrawal of Yugoslavian troops that were repressing civilians, safe return of refugees and initiation of a meaningful dialogue with the Kosovar Albanians.

United Nations resolutions, using such unenforceable words as "immediate" and "meaningful" always seemed to me to be so much hot air, but this one had already prompted the NATO Council to the kind of action only international bureaucrats understand – the approval of first an ACTWARN and then an ACTREQ, and finally, on the night we arrived in the Balkans, of an ACTORD. The way I understood it, the first simply hinted to Milosevic that unless 1199 was complied with, NATO was unofficially considering action; the second made it official that NATO might act and the third replaced the "might" with "would." While these acronyms draw ho-hum responses from the public, they represent hard fought and often bitter battles among the sixteen NATO nations. As I lay there in that Zagreb bed, although I sensed the importance of this new action, I did not expect it to produce concrete results. That there *could* be air strikes against Milosevic four days from now if he didn't begin to implement 1199 – what did that mean? The 96 hours of grace gave Holbrook the chance to force Milosevic to do the right thing, but there was a lot of stuff in 1199 that was hard to pin down – how immediate a cease fire and what was a cease fire anyway? which troops, how many, how fast, and how would we know? And hell would freeze over before the Serbs and Albanians initiated a "meaningful dialogue." I doubted that there would be either NATO bombing or a resolution of the Kosovo situation for a long time to come. But I was willing to play the game. Dick's game.

"That gives us 96 hours in Bosnia," I said to Mary, as we turned the TV off.

"And we'll ask the embassy, tomorrow, if it's safe to go," she added.

"For Dick. Right."

But I knew we'd go, no matter what they said. You can't prepare your heart for Sarajevo and go to Palermo instead.

The woman at the U.S. consulate, the next morning, was perplexed by our question.

"Why *wouldn't* you go to Sarajevo? If you want to go – go! That's up to you."

"That was embarrassing!" said Mary, back on the sidewalk.

"Remember, we did it for Dick. Let's document it with a photo," I said and Mary posed beneath the American flag. As I slipped my camera back into my bag a man who had been lounging against the wall came forward.

"I have to take that film. You can't take pictures of the embassy."

"Why didn't you tell me that before I took the picture? Who are you anyway?"

"Head of security.'"

"Am I a threat to your security?"

"This is among the top ten most vulnerable U.S. embassies," he said, reminding me of that world only vaguely connected to our own, where embassies in Nairobi and Dar Es Salaam had recently been blown up and scores of people killed, "and we have our rules." He opened my camera and tugged at the film, which didn't budge. He handed it back.

"I can't get this out, but it's exposed, so take it and get out of here."

"Right."

"I would have expected the head of security to know how to remove film from a camera." I muttered to Mary as we hurried off.

"Why?" said Mary, "If he thinks we're a security threat, he can't be that bright."

"Maybe he had a destroyed-film quota to fill." I said. In the Chicago of the 1950's the issuance of traffic tickets was driven by the quota system and if you were smart, on the last night of the quota period, you stayed off the streets.

We had a piece of business in Zagreb before we left – to deliver the typewriter to a woman Mary sponsored through an American organization called *Women For Women*, which funnels contributions from the United States into the hands of women that are struggling to survive in war torn countries. Mary wanted to visit their offices in both Zagreb and Sarajevo. Thus we took our first step into the world of war.

We sat in the single room in the school for blind and retarded children where Ana lived with her blind husband Pere and his three blind children. The school was in a lovely shaded residential area, and Croatian President Tudjman's home could be seen through the trees. Ana was our age but unlike us, she was a saint. Jammed in the little room, knees touching knees, she served us our second gritty cup of Croatian coffee (what we call *Turkish* unless we're on Halsted Street in Chicago, where it is called *Greek*) made on a hotplate, orange juice poured from a carton and some packaged cookies, as she told her story through Milan, our translator.

They had come there from Vukovar. I remembered Vukovar from my reading as one of the earliest of Milosevic's hell holes. Ana was on her way to sainthood even before the war, when she married Pere to care for his children after their own mother died, and they lived comfortably in a large middle-class house. We looked at the remnants of that life, a bulky photo album, full of memories of a normal happy life. She had been much heavier, older-looking, then. The war that had done such damage to her heart and soul had been good to her body. The pictures showed a woman very different from the woman who showed them.

The Serbian army had an easy march into Vukovar, less than 40 miles from the Serbian border and closer to Belgrade than to Zagreb. They came to claim the Krajina region for their own, believing, as the Nazis had done in the late 1930's, that where people of their blood line lived, they should be part of the motherland. And there were plenty of Serbs in Vukovar, having lived peaceably with their Croatian neighbors for many years. Milosevic did more than go after the valuable natural resources of the region; he wanted all the Croatians out – that was the ethnic cleansing part.

The astonishing thing about the Balkan wars was how easy it was to convince people that if they didn't act against their neighbors, take away their homes and livelihood or even lives, their neighbors would do those things to them. But that's what Milosevic did and did well, first in Croatia and then in Bosnia, replacing former bonds of friendship and community with suspicion and hate. It's a modern form of warfare.

Centuries before, the Ottoman Turks had marched through parts of the Balkans without driving the people out – to make their lives easier the people had simply converted to Islam or, in cases where their faith meant more to them, Christians stayed on as people of lesser status. But today's leaders know that enemies in their midst can cause trouble down the line and it was easier for Milosevic to eradicate potential trouble makers in Vukovar – the Roman Catholic Croatians. Likewise in Kosovo, even though the Muslim Albanians vastly outnumbered the Serbs, he was apparently determined to drive the non-Serbs out.

Ana and Pere, their friends and family, had no sense of that kind of trouble brewing in Vukovar, where they lived in a world as orderly as Mary's in New Hampshire or mine in Indiana. At first they ignored the echo of faraway gunfire at dusk. Gradually the grenades exploded at closer range and then there were soldiers in the street, gunning down people from the neighborhood in front of their own house, and mortars came out of the sky to destroy single residences, then entire blocks. A full blown nightmare erupted when a Serbian neighbor set fire to their home. After that, Pere took the children to Zagreb while Ana stayed in the war torn city, living in a nearby basement and baking bread for Croatian fighters, for three and a half months. Toward the end of fighting she was captured and put in jail for 20 days, but finally got away to Zagreb.

She told her story in a monotone, as Milan translated and Pere sat mute behind her, tears in his eyes.

"The women may survive this war," Milan said to us in English, "but not the men. They lose everything they have spent their lives building. The woman's work is always there – caring for the children, feeding the men. The only thing for men to do is to fight to stay alive. And while we may have won the war, all these people have left is their lives- they have no future, no hope of rebuilding what they had. You should see Vukovar – it will be years before it is livable again."

"Won't they be able to go back?"

"Not likely. Their lives beyond this room are over, and they know it," Milan said.

Our expressions of sympathy were stifled by the deep sadness that pervaded our little group and after drinking our coffee and taking a cookie or two, we left.

They took the typewriter without comment. I listened for a thank you in the languages spoken that day, but heard none, and complained to Mary later.

"They feel entitled," she said briskly, "and they have that right."

Whatever that meant.

Mary and Ana

We had been taken to Ana's by Judy and Milan, who had a story of their own. Judy, an American nurse and ardent Roman Catholic, had traveled to Croatia in the early 90's to visit the famous shrine of Marija Bistrica. The country had just declared independence and been invaded by Serbia, however, and she became aware of the brutal fighting on the front, where the militarily unprepared Croatians were battling for their lives. Judy was determined to stay, found a way to get to the front, and worked there as a nurse for the rest of the war. It was there she met Milan, a military commander. Their photo album commemorating that time was full of faces who had experienced suffering and death. The two of them had married after the war and she had become the Croatian representative of *Women for Women*. They both spent all their time helping those who had been hurt by the war.

"If you are free tomorrow," Milan said to us as we left Ana's, "there is a place I'd like to take you."

He picked us up at the hotel at 8 AM and drove us deep into the Slavonia region, in the direction of Vukovar. By ten we were sitting in Milka and Ljubo's Covac home, sipping gritty Serbian (indistinguishable from Croatian) coffee from dainty cups and homemade plum brandy from robin's egg blue, thimble-sized glasses. We sat crowded in the parlor, heated by a wood stove and decorated with photographs that chronicled their tragic lives. Behind us on the sofa lay their 23-year old retarded daughter, sucking on a coke bottle.

"We say, "said Milan, "that Croatians serve food to visitors but in a Serbian home, they serve you drink."

Milka and Ljubo were Serbian. The coffee and brandy were luxuries for this couple, who had no income and lived on what they raised. The ducks and chickens roaming in the yard provided eggs and meat. The pig fattening in the shed would be slaughtered and salted away by the time the snows came. Even the two tethered dogs had a role to play – as guards. It still was not safe to live in Covac.

War had destroyed most of the town where they lived – roofs blasted away, walls collapsed, windows shattered and wind and rain forcing entry into still furnished, wall-papered rooms. The few habitable homes were surrounded by piles of rubble and overgrown fields. Although it was mostly populated by Serbian people, they had lived comfortably within the boundaries of Croatia. But when Croatia declared independence from the rest of Yugoslavia in the early 90's, they had suffered the fate of Vukovar – the Serbian army had crossed the border to capture this town and much of the rich Croatian territory known as Slavonia. Milka's relatives, living in Covac, were among the Serbs in whose name this conquest occurred.

Milan, who had driven us out from Zagreb on this Sunday morning, first came to Covac as leader of a military brigade in the Croatian army, marching from Zagreb to recapture Slavonia. And so they did, shooting, bombing, mining, killing and destroying toward the east as the Serbians had done before them toward the west. Thus a brief but ugly war between Serbia and Croatia was fought where we now sat and sipped our slivovitz.

"When my troops arrived in Covac," said Milan, "most civilians had left the town. The Serbian front line was in that field," pointing across the road, "fighting was fierce and by the time we drove them back the town was a shambles. I asked my men to bring me the few people who were left."

As he told the story he translated for Milka who leaned forward toward us eagerly and often interrupted, frequently with laughter. These people were not defeated, as Ana and Pere had been.

"You told them not to worry," said Milka, "that they would be treated well. And they were."

"Two old women in black stood in the back and never said a word. I don't think they liked me." He glanced sideways at Milka.

"They didn't. One was my mother," said Milka.

"I couldn't forget those women and when the war was over I came back to see if they were still alive."

"My mother remembered you all right, as 'that little guy with eyes like a snake!'

Today his eyes held too much twinkle for a snake. I could not imagine him as a military commander.

"Her mother is dead now," Milan said, "this is her house."

Milan kept coming back to Covac and when Milka and Ljubo returned, the friendship between the Serbian couple and the Croatian soldier began. Judy enrolled Milka in *Women for Women*, giving her $20 a month.

"It's the only cash they get. There are no jobs for miles around," said Milan.

We had joined him on his monthly trip to bring the money.

"We are told in America," Mary said, "that Serbs and Croats don't get along, because of ancient hatreds."

Milka smiled and left the room, returning with a U-shaped symbol pinned to her dress.

"I am now Ustache!"

"Oh yes, and I am Chetnik," growled Milan, making a fierce face. They hugged each other, laughing.

These two were making sport of ugly stuff. In this part of the Balkans a reference to Ustache and Chetniks can be asking for trouble. When Serbians want to conjure up an image of the Croats who slaughtered thousands of Serbs during World War II, they call them "Ustache," the name of the vicious pro-Nazi element. The Serbian image that the Croatians despise is the sadistic Chetnik guerilla from the same period, from Tito's little band of desperados. These names and images were revived in the 1990's to stir up bitterness between Croats and Serbs. But this Croatian soldier and his Serbian friend, poking fun by reversing the images, were having none of it.

"Our families suffered in World War II, hers from the Ustache and mine from the Chetniks, but we can't afford to live in the past. It's like your cowboys and Indians," Milan told us, pulling out imaginary six-shooters and aiming them at Milka, "bang, bang."

But Milan listened intently and no longer joked when Ljubo talked about the lingering bitterness and paranoia of others in the town. Some neighbors charged that the horseshoe nailed above their door was Ustache symbolism and so Milka let it slip sideways, spilling out the luck, as my New England grandfather would have said.

We Yankee farmers shared this superstition with our eastern European counterparts and other things as well. Before Ustache and Chetniks were creating a living hell for the parents of Milan and Milka, their lives were much like ours. All through the summer my mother canned the produce of our garden. We slaughtered a pig and the cows provided milk and cream and butter. Such farms in the United States are largely gone today, replaced by corporate giants and hobbyists. I, one of the latter, keep goats. We talked of it.

"I'd love a goat," sighed Milka, "but we can't afford one. Do you make cheese?"

"Yes. My goat delivered two kids last spring. I have more milk than I need and plenty to make cheese. I wish I could send the one kid to you."

"How wonderful that would be!" said Milka, "I barter now for milk and cheese, and with a goat, I could make money, selling to others."

"Forget that!" said Milan, "Getting a goat across international borders is impossible."

It was all wrong that I should have too many goats and she have none! The animals were an amusement for me, but the goat Milka did not have could make a big difference in a life that could not afford the luxury of hobbies! How unequal our lives were, in neither case deserved but rather, an accident of our births. I began to feel uncomfortable about my goats.

Before we left Milan took us to visit two brothers who lived with their mother up the road.

"This woman stood with Milka's mother, that day, calling me a snake," he laughed as we sat before the bed in which she lay. A chicken nestled by her side among the old quilts. He held the old woman's hand and they spoke softly to each other for several minutes. Mary and I watched in amazement as the chicken ruffled her feathers, squawked and deposited a damp warm egg among the blankets.

Soon after, as Milan talked with one of the sons and I shifted restlessly from foot to foot, Mary wandered off across the fields. Milan spotted her and snapped at me.

"Get her back here fast! There are mines out there. Believe me, I know."

"Mary, we're leaving," I shouted, a bit too frantically. Maybe Dick was right.

We returned to Milka's and as we climbed into the car, she brought gifts: freshly made bread and garden preserves for Milan and a bottle of homemade slivovitz for Mary and me.

"My god, Milan, how can they part with these?"

"Giving gifts is important to them."

"Can I give her something?" I whispered, getting out my wallet.

"Only if you want to insult them." He pushed my hand back in my purse.

We said goodbye and thank you – *kvala* – and were on our way.

"What do you think?" asked Milan, his black eyes darting back and forth from the road to me, sitting beside him.

"How hard they are working, to build back up from nothing!"

"It's not easy. Serbians are at the bottom of the list in getting help from the Croatian government."

"What awes me most is you and Milka, Croat and Serb, what good friends you are! It is the stuff that will bring peace to the former Yugoslavia."

"We have to get past the war."

"I wanted to give them something, they are so special. Why wouldn't you let me?"

"They would have seen it as payment for their gifts, and that would hurt. You Americans think money solves everything. It doesn't."

On the drive back, as Mary dozed in the back seat, I was still brooding about my goats. I hated the idea of having goats as long as Milka didn't. It didn't make much sense, but I was obsessed. I told Milan, we talked, and together hatched a plan. I'd give Milan the money, he'd go to the animal market and between the two of us, Milka would have her goat. It seemed to me a real, an authentic thing to do. I didn't feel good but I felt better.

CHAPTER 3

SARAJEVO HOLIDAY

We got the last two seats on the midday Air Croatia flight to Sarajevo. The passengers were bulky grim faced men, a willowy blonde who disappeared into the cockpit, and us. My somersaulting stomach refused the offered cheese sandwich – thanks to my pre-trip reading, I was back in the war. Landing in Sarajevo, back then, planes dove in screaming descent onto the runway, to escape Serbian fire from the surrounding hills. My ears and heart were ready to explode during the final leg and through what turned out to be an uneventful landing.

We stood uncomfortably in the slow passport control line in a room more like an army barracks than an airport. Mary surveyed our mostly black-leather-jacketed companions. None smiled, most hadn't shaved and a few had scars. Gangster types who scared me.

"Which one of these guys do you think is going to take us hostage?" Mary asked me loudly, turning about to look them over.

"Shut up," I whispered.

Dick was right – she was going to get us killed.

As inept at finding our bags as in Zagreb, we finally spotted them inexplicably sitting alone in a corner. We shoved into the line that processed them through an x-ray machine. X-ray transition from airplane to city, where the city, not the plane, was the dangerous place. Such oddities added to my unease.

The airport had no signs, no customer service representatives, nothing but cold, dirt and a door to the outside. We went through it and waved at what looked like a taxi. It was, and the driver spoke some English.

"Holiday Inn," I told him. Saying the words gave me a thrill. We were actually going to the famous Sarajevo motel – it was expensive, but we had to stay one night there, for history's sake. Our driver, to my surprise, showed no interest in our destination.

As we swung out from the airport, around a cemetery and onto the main road into Sarajevo, I was as frightened as if the war was still going on. The books I'd read came to life as we moved down the so-called Sniper Alley that runs five miles along the narrow valley of the Miljacka River which flowed along the highway on our right. Beyond it were the hills and mountains that rise steeply from the valley floor, and between those hills and the highway were blocks and blocks of bombed out buildings, demolished by those guns that a few years ago had jettisoned 4,000 shells a day into this densely populated valley, killing 10,615 citizens, among them 1,601 children, from 1991 to 1995. We didn't speak for staring at buildings whose history we knew – the burned out building of the publisher that had continued to print newspapers in the basement even as the building above burned, the state museum, hit by 420 shells, now wreathed in plastic sheeting to replace its shattered windows . . .

Then, before us was the infamous Holiday Inn.

"Ugly, huh?" our driver said.

Not to my eyes. In shades of yellow-orange and brown, disproportionately rising in cantilevered blocks, the plaster had been repaired, the outside painted, and windows replaced. It was a thing of beauty, a miracle, this transformation of the bombed-out shell where terrified Sarajevans had escaped to safety and stranded journalists had lived without heat or electricity. We faced the eastern side which Serbian gunners had pounded mercilessly day and night. I looked back across the river – no threat in those hills today. Time had erased its history, wiped the slate clean. Ghosts seldom linger at sites of historical import but I had expected them to in this place – I needed them somehow.

We walked dazed into the glass-sided atrium, where white coated waiters served drinks to a number of solitary men who lounged about on Roche Bobois-style couches, half shielded from the reception area by potted palms.

Life-threatening races across this lobby? Desperate people risking death to get through these doors? I was Alice, walking through the looking glass, departing reality as I entered this Holiday Inn on Marshall Tito Street. That old Holiday Inn that had been real, moments before, became a dream, a memory, replaced by this new slick, doppelganger.

I simply couldn't, didn't want to make it work, the transition from then to now. I had come to kneel before the altar of an imagining that was slipping away as the neatly uniformed clerk asked for our names and passports.

On the third floor of our Holiday Inn, as we let ourselves into a color coordinated room with an electronic key, we glimpsed two burly pistol-equipped men guarding the door of a room down the hall.

"Bodyguards?" whispered Mary.

That was better. We were where we thought we were.

Sitting in the lobby lounge, an hour later, two Sarajevans joined us, the mother and brother of a friend of a friend of Mary's. It was for the boy that she had brought the boots and to whom she handed them now, as they made the preliminary small talk and I looked around. The spire of a mosque was silhouetted dramatically by the setting sun on the hills outside. A short pudgy man emerged from a conference room surrounded by a bevy of bodyguards. Most of the guys lounging around us leapt to their feet and formed a phalanx as he moved rapidly across the lobby toward the smoked-glass limousine that was pulling up to the door.

"Carlos Westendorp," said the boy.

I knew who he was – the very high "High Representative" of western governments in Bosnia. Things were falling into place. The past was not so far away, after all.

"How was it for you during the war," asked Mary of the mother, Melica.

The three of them – there was a father/husband too – had lived there for the four long years, and she slowly began to talk about their lives during that time, full of hunger, fear, danger, misery of every kind, as well as courage and a plucky determination to survive. It was hard to connect this cultivated refined woman and her son with the harsh events she described.

We let our book learning inform our own remarks. I made reference to the Serbs, the enemy.

"Don't forget," the son said, "*we* are Serbian."

"Huh?"

It was not an easy thing to grasp.

"But if *you* are Serbians, I asked, "who are the *they?*"

'The bad Serbians," he laughed. And therein lay the key.

Several nights later we had dinner at an upscale underground restaurant, Jez, where sometimes the American Ambassador ate, where John Malkovich's autographed picture hung, and where, this night, a group of exuberant Italian soldiers lined a long table. We sat across from two American expatriates whose anger flowed out onto their Veal Picata and Slovenian Riesling.

"It's not about ancient animosities between Serbs and Bosnians," Colleen said, "it's about good and evil."

Both she and her friend Manuela wore their passions on their sleeves and bombarded us with their view of the Sarajevo world: Bosnians, everyone who lived in Bosnia and was a victim of the war (certainly Melica and her Serbian family would qualify) were good. The attackers, those minions of Milosevic, now lurking threateningly just beyond the border in Dayton's newly created enclave, the Serb Republika (RS), were evil. Almost everyone else lay closer to the evil than the good. The two women hated: America for its indifference to the current suffering, the United Nations for having refused to stop the war, the UNHCR for not repatriating fast enough, Richard Holbrook for the inadequate Dayton Accord. The list was long and I suspected that it included middle aged American women who came to snoop. They needed a release for their rage at the entire world for not helping the suffering people that they worked with – the people of Sarajevo, who had endured so much.

Among their obsessions, however, were issues that caught our attention. Two things, they told us, must be accomplished before there is true peace, before the international troops could go home. The International Criminal Tribunal for Yugoslavia (ICTY) established by the UN in The Hague in 1993 must provide justice and the hundreds of thousands of displaced people must be able to go home.

"Justice can be just another word for revenge," said Mary. "Would you settle for a Peace Commission like South Africa had?"

"Without justice there will never be peace," answered Colleen, "if a man has killed your son, you want him to pay for it. Whatever word you use – justice or revenge – you cannot live at peace without it."

"And so the killing is perpetrated," said Mary. "What happens to forgiveness?"

"Easy for you to say that word," said Manuela, "but not possible for them."

We learned a lot from these two women who so ably defended the cause they served. When the bill came they looked the other way as Mary and I dug deep for the heavy drop of cash required by the pricey place that had been selected by our guests.

"That took some nerve," I said after they left. "They didn't even offer."

"They all feel so damned entitled," sighed Mary, "and I suppose they are."

I didn't get it – not at all. No one was entitled to anything; you earned it or were willing to go without.

We had moved to another, cheaper hotel, where hot water from the boiler took 20 minutes, each morning, to reach our room, too long for Mary, who first called the desk to complain and then took it out on the plumbing fixtures. By the time I headed for the shower, postponing as long as I could, the hot water had made it through the pipes. Mary was already on the phone, confirming the details of her tightly scheduled agenda.

Our first stop was Sarajevo's Bjelave orphanage, where 115 of the estimated 3,300 parentless children scattered around Bosnia, (most of whom live with friends and relatives) were surrounded by attentive staff and piles of toys. Our guide was Julia, a 30-year old British volunteer whose basic expenses were paid by her church, back home, was learning Bosnian and planned to stay until there was no more work to do. Mary told her about the rumors of rape babies being ostracized but, according to Julia, the children were well cared for and loved, although they could have used more staff. The distress I had expected to feel gave way to admiration, for the clean bright rooms, the smiling children and the hard working staff. Above all, I admired Julia.

We met many others like her, among the ten thousand foreigners, 1,600 of whom are Americans, who had come – from Ireland, England, Norway, the Middle East, Japan – to help put the city back upon its feet. We visited the IRC, UNICEF, and WHO, all appointments Mary had scheduled in advance, along with local agencies that we discovered as we went. Everyone was friendly and eager to talk about their work and at the end of the day we, who mostly listened, were worn out.

The city was a monument to the war, and the long hikes led by Melica detoured us around piles of rubble, over ripped up pavements, and past empty shells of buildings. We stepped gingerly around the *Sarajevo Roses* that were everywhere – a name the locals gave to the scars of bomb bursts that marred the city sidewalks, painted red in memory of the ones who died on those spots. Fear remained palpable in the city – fear that the pain and suffering would never go away.

There was a demonstration in the street one day, a marching of thick-set middle-aged men. Taxi drivers, Melica told us, because the previous night a driver took a passenger across the border to the Serb Republika (RS) and did not return; he was found dead in his cab. But we two Americans felt no fear. Every day we saw dozens of the international military force, a presence 30,000 strong, of whom 6,000 were Americans. The closest Mary came to danger was when she walked through the door of a mosque as an old man shouted and waved his arms at her.

"What was his problem?" she asked, back with me on the sidewalk.

"Women aren't allowed in mosques," I said.

"Tough!" she said.

Dick would have felt validated.

We had lunch with Ann Sides, the American Counsel General, who had been much amused when we went to register, as we had promised Dick we would.

"We don't get many folks who holiday in Sarajevo," she said, commenting on how we had identified our visit.

Ann took us to the Kafe Picerija INDI, where we shared a pepperoni and mushroom pizza, and she talked about her former posting in Belgrade. She was there in 1992, when the official U.S. policy was neutrality, which we all agreed was the official word for indifference, as the outrages escalated. She watched from the bridge over a viaduct near her apartment as masses of Serbian troops marched off to decimate Vukovar, an act which Milosevic's government denied. She and her husband were stunned and their Serbians friends were ashamed. Then she was sent to Zagreb, where a writer-lawyer came to her with an ugly story of a fat rendering plant in Brcko, on the Sava River, where flesh of unknown origin was being melted down by Serbs. The details of his story brought home to her the monstrosities that were happening around her and she looked for a way to help.

At that time the United States did not accept refugees from this terrible war (one of our many acts of indifference growing out of Secretary of State James Baker's argument that "we have no dogs in this fight") and when she could no longer bear refusing visas to the desperate people around her she successfully got the "Eastern European" immigration quota into the United States to be applied to Croatians rather than Russians.

"If I get into heaven," she said, "that'll be why."

We'd met a lot of people, that week, who had the credentials to pass through that gate. An odd way to measure worth – a measure that I would fall short of but Mary would probably not.

'What about the Kosovars," I asked, "will the U.S. open their doors to them?"

"Kosovars are as likely to qualify for immigration to the United States as to be struck by lightning."

Ann had come recently to Bosnia and was getting up to speed.

"I'm reading *End Game*," she said, "and I find it unbearable."

To Ann, to me and to anyone who knew the story of Srebrenica, the whole world, including the three of us eating pizza, shared a small piece of monster Mladić's guilt. How could the survivors of Srebrenica – the women and children – bear to live on the same planet with us.

That very night we met one of them.

Melica, who would certainly have been a member of the League of Women Voters if she had lived in my home town, took us to a meeting of *ZeneZenama* (Women to Women), a group of women who came together weekly to solve the immediate problems of their lives. Zilha personified the displacement problems that Colleen and Manuela spoke so intensely about. Forced from her home in a suburb during the war, she lived in the Sarajevan apartment of a Serbian family who fled before the siege and now wished to return. She, in turn, wanted to go back to her own home, but its occupants, Muslims who fled the Serbian invasion of their village in what is now the Serb Republika, had no place to go, themselves. The government of the RS was making no effort to allow non-Serbs to return to their homes and it was too dangerous for the

Muslims who lived in Zilha's house to force their way back in – making them leave would be driving them to their deaths. We heard several similar stories that night.

Among these women was Mina, one of a group of sixteen women who moved to nearby Ilidza when they were driven out of Srebrenica. While the others talked freely – they were an educated, articulate group – she sat quietly. She was a grey, gentle little woman, in her 30's perhaps, to whom everyone was kind. I have forgotten the other faces, but I remember hers. Being in the room with her froze me up. Talk about entitlement – I was feeling the reverse. Getting through the gates of heaven was out of the question – I was unentitled to everything I had and these women did not. Even – especially – the intangibles.

"We're tired of knocking on the door," Tamara said, "and asking for our civil rights." No need to say thank you for what you'd earned twice over. Mary had understood what I had not.

NATO's 96-hour deadline came and went, at three AM on the fourth day we were in Sarajevo. NATO's General Wesley Clark reported, as we showered and dressed to CNN, that while there was not yet full compliance with conditions agreed upon, the deadline for air strikes was extended to October 27th. Beyond that, we were told, "there will be no further extension."

"Yeah, right," I muttered. Mary, who was on the phone complaining about the lack of hot water, had nothing to say.

That day Melica took us to the old town, telling us more pieces of her story as we sat in an outdoor café eating Cevapcici and drinking gritty portions of the ubiquitous Balkan coffee, now labeled *Bosnian*. Later we wandered in the warm October sunlight along the river, spanned with charming bridges at every intersection.

Photographers set up cameras here," she said, pointing, "then hid behind that building and watched when people made a dash across. If a sniper was watching at the same time and had good enough aim, they'd capture the 'live shot of death' that would make them famous."

We'd heard these stories but thought they were exaggerations.

"It's true," she said, "and sometimes journalists – she named a Russian one – would hang out with the snipers and try their own hand at killing us."

Unbelievable! Melica, who with her son and husband, had been among the living targets as they hurried through the streets trying to stay alive, shopping for food or gathering wood for the stove, didn't care if we believed them or not. After four years in that city, dodging bullets and bombs, she had seen the blackness in men's souls that we could only wonder about. We passed the burned out post office and stopped by the remnants of the national library, where a million books had been destroyed.

"There used to be a plaque here, on this corner," said Melica, "to commemorate June 28, 1914 when Gavrilo Princip assassinated Franz Ferdinand and his wife."

Princip had been born in Bosnia of Serbian parents and had killed the Prince in a Serbian cause. His act had set off World War I, the first great conflagration of a very conflagratious century.

"Do they think they can change history by destroying its mementos?" asked Melica angrily, her Serbian genes giving her the right to chastise those who could not distinguish between the present and the past. By such reasoning Mary, with her Calvinistic Scottish genes, would have been blasting out my Catholic Stuart brains.

There may have been times when she wanted to. I spent far more time lying about the hotel room than did she. I took a pass one afternoon and read while Mary had one more interview. When she returned my mind was on food.

"How about that seafood restaurant tonight," – a little white tablecloth establishment had caught my eye. "And a bottle of that good Slovenian white wine?"

"I'm not hungry," she said, but let me drag her off anyway.

I paid more attention to what we ate and drank than she considered fitting. It was something that Dick and I had in common and drove her crazy. The three of us had once gone to Chicago-land's elegant Le Français Restaurant where Mary vomited up her cherries jubilee in the chic ladies' room, in what I suspected was a personal comment on our wasting two hours fawning over ultra-expensive food.

But in our view of non-eating experiences, she and I were as one.

One evening we wandered alone down Marshall Tito Street, within a river of lively handsome young people who filled the bars and cafes with laughter, talk and music. The windows of the shops were full of merchandise. Mary grabbed my arm.

"Look."

The window was full of boots of every size and shape at prices more reasonable than in the States. I understood.

One of our visits was to poor John Michel Godsticker, head of the UNHCR – United Nationals High Commission on Refugees. Poor, I say, because he was overwhelmed, both with his job and the conditions under which he worked. We climbed six flights of stairs to sit with him in a very cold office amid a thunderstorm, as he described the mission of the UNHCR to "lead and coordinate international action for the world-wide protection of refugees and the resolution of refugee problems." The international law that the agency implements is the 1951 Geneva Convention on refugees, updated in 1967 and signed by 145 nations, a precious hard fought-for international document that governs national behavior. In most places it does a bang up job but the Kosovar refugees in Bosnia presented some special problems.

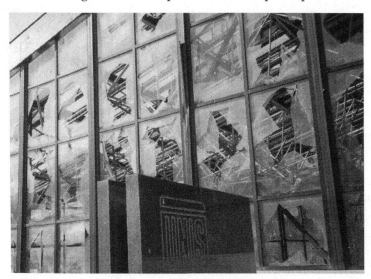
UN building in Sarajevo

John Michel told us the UN had recently estimated that 230,000 of the original two million Kosovars had been forcibly "displaced" from their homes (NATO was now estimating that number to be 400,000), and while two thirds of them were still somewhere in Kosovo the remainder had scattered to other countries.

Already the numbers pouring into Bosnia were more than John Michel's agency could handle: eight thousand had registered with the refugee office in Sarajevo, with the numbers increasing every day. Twenty four hundred had arrived in September alone. Many came with the hope that they could continue west, but most western countries refused to allow resettlement programs out of Bosnia. They were stuck in this country indefinitely and although the 1951 Convention gave primary responsibility for protecting the refugees to the host governments, Bosnia was too new a state to have signed on. Struggling to insure its own survival, dealing with asylum seekers from other countries was not a priority in Sarajevo.

We had our own proof of that. When we asked Melica about the nearby Kosovar refugee camp, that long-suffering gentle woman had snapped, "Those Kosovars? Why did they come here anyway!"

She sensed how little sympathy there is in the world and resented any one's taking away her city's rightful share.

The Refugee Conventions expect the host country to provide the basic necessities until the area from which people have fled is secure enough to accept them back "with dignity," but John Michel told us the Sarajevan authorities were both uncooperative and ill-equipped to take over the camps the UNHCR was setting up. Five hundred empty beds were available in their transit centers but the Bosnian Federation denied the Kosovars their use, keeping them available for their own refugees, expected to return from temporary asylum in Germany, which had helped prepare those centers. Thousands of Kosovar refugees would be in Bosnia indefinitely, during which time they couldn't travel, work, or go to school beyond the 4th grade – if there were even a school to go to.

We had an open day that Mary hadn't programmed and were torn between two plans: to take the train to Tuzla or to visit the Kosovar refugee camp outside the city. Colleen had encouraged us to do the latter and although in the end she couldn't bear to make the trip herself she pointed the way that took us to where I found myself, that Sunday afternoon, staring into the beautiful smiling face of a girl called Henkelinda who was telling me she spoke English.

"Please, please come see my mama," she said.

Reluctantly I let her lead me away from Mary, off to one of the tents. Inside, a sad-eyed, soft bodied woman, a small boy clinging to her skirt, pulled herself up from a chair. Two scrawny boyish kids in shorts and tee shirts with close cropped hair stood nearby.

"My mother Dyke and my sisters, Nika and Hita, six and eight years old."

"Who's this?" I bent toward the toddler. He scowled and ducked behind his mother.

"Gufim. My other brother is Nimi – twelve."

Another girl appeared.

"My sister Nare, fifteen. I am seventeen."

Nare's hair, like her mothers, was black and straight, chopped short, her dull eyes shadowed by heavy brows, her face expressionless.

"Seven of you in this tent?"

Six cots were jammed among the scattered clothing and bags in the shadows beyond.

"Gufim sleeps with Mama."

"Please, have an Albanian coffee with us," said Henkelinda, pulling me down onto a wooden bench.

It was more plea than invitation. I settled reluctantly beside her, across from Dyke, with Hita and Nika cross-legged at our feet. My life was about to change.

Nare slipped away and by the time she reappeared, carrying a small steaming pot, Henkelinda had unearthed a green and yellow hand-crocheted cover and with it transformed a packing crate into a coffee table. Nare filled three fluted paper cups, the gargle cups in dentists' offices, presented them to

Henkelinda, her mother and me and joined her sisters on the floor. Gufim sulked behind his mother's chair.

I yielded to the coffee – hot and sweet and good and if it was also gritty, I didn't notice. Its offering transformed this corner of the dirty camp into an intimate home.

"Would you tell me your story?" I asked Henkelinda. And slowly she did, seducing me out of my world into theirs, managing in her mixed up English to describe the events that led them to this United Nations' refugee camp. It was a sad and deeply moving account and not knowing what else to do when she was done, I got up awkwardly and pulling out my wallet, stuffed a 20 DM note into Henkelinda's hand. But the minute I did it I was terribly ashamed – it was as if I could buy escape back to the safe haven of my life, as if I could walk away from their lives as one would a movie theater, wiping one's eyes during the quick passage from fantasy to the day-to-day. How cheaply I valued their lives with that pathetic bill.

"I must go to find my friend," I said to Dyke and left, but Henkelinda was not so easily dismissed. She clutched my arm, and Hita trotted behind as we entered the main factory building, where a sea of gray blankets covered makeshift beds constructed from wooden two-by-fours and overlaid with thin mattresses. Many of the thick blankets hung from ropes, to give a little privacy, breaking up the open factory floor. People and their smells were everywhere. Some slept, some lay staring into space, others talked quietly among themselves. Some watched us walk the aisles, most turned away as we got close. More than half of the people in the camp were family groups, but there were many single men in their late teens and early twenties, the military age. I found Mary in conversation with a group of these. Actually, she was in conversation with just one, Esad, whose English was far better than the rest.

Esad had been in school when things in Kosovo got hot and, learning that his name was on a list to be picked up for questioning, he'd headed for the border. Not inclined to be a fighter, on either side, his college antics in defiance of the Serbian oppressions had gotten him in trouble. The others, who had crossed the border for similar reasons, gathered close by, trying to follow the conversation, interjecting in Albanian and Serbian. Mary was asking them about the camp.

Twenty six portable toilets, two drinking water taps, eight showers were set up, not much for more than 1,200 people. The medical clinics were staffed by *Medecins sans Frontieres*, using medicines provided by *Pharmaciens sans Frontieres*. Some cook stoves were available but food came in, two hot meals each day, from outside contractors. Beds were constructed from wooden two-by-fours, equipped with thin mattresses and the ubiquitous grey blankets.

They were given clothes enough but the women were desperate for sanitary napkins and diapers.

Henkelinda whispered that a Croatian organization had sent seven cartons of tampons but the women didn't know how to use them.

"Why don't you explain it to them?" I asked.

"How could I – I am a virgin." she said. Female anatomy was not among her areas of expertise.

The biggest problem in the camp, Esad told Mary, was that they had nothing to fill their time. The only activity occurred each evening, when they gathered around a radio for news from home.

"Why don't you start a school for the children?" Mary asked.

"With what?" asked Esad, "For a school you need books, paper, pencils . . ."

"We'll get you some," said Mary.

When we left the camp, two hours later, we rummaged through the few open stores on Marshal Tito Street for books, school supplies, balls and toys for the children to play with. We bought as much as our arms could carry and our budgets would allow and early the next morning returned to the camp. But as too many children snatched and clawed at too few things disputes arose and the situation soured. I felt the worse for doing it.

Henkelinda did not leave my side that morning and Hita was always in the group that tagged along. The children kicked and tossed the balls, we talked and laughed and put our arms around each other to pose for photos in the soft warm October sunshine. They all talked of the winter that was close at hand with its promised bitter cold. This place – the factory and the tents – was not heated. I stopped by the tent to shake Dyke's limp hand, made lifeless by her deep despair. At the end of the day we said goodbye, this time for good. Our flight was the next day.

Henkelinda and I with others in the Coca Cola Camp

I simply walked away leaving my new friend with no place to go, no thing to do, no life to live except the one of refugee. It was an accident of birth, hers in a war zone, mine more fortunate. But another accident had linked our lives and the sharp edge between the two worlds cut deeply as I stepped from her world back into mine.

"I won't forget you," I promised Henkelinda and got into the taxi where Mary was waiting. I was crying. Mary gave me a disapproving look.

"Whatever are you crying for?" she asked, "This is no worse than so much else we've seen and heard."

"I guess my soul got overloaded," I said.

"Surely it's bigger than that."

"You didn't hear the story of Henkelinda's family, Mary."

"Tell me," she said, and so I did.

CHAPTER 4

HENKELINDA'S STORY

"The war began for me," Henkelinda said as I sipped my coffee from the fluted paper cup, "in the middle of the school day, June 30, 1998."

My words, not hers. Her English couldn't handle complete sentences. It didn't surprise me, at the time, that I understood so much of what she said because I was busy filling in the gaps and enhancing her simple verbs and monosyllabic nouns with images of my own, coloring them with my imaginings. I was enchanted with this girl and so intently did I watch and listen that her words and gestures created a rich dramatic story that I thought I understood.

She began by talking about that June day four months earlier, when she was sitting with two dozen other 11th graders on the floor in her teacher's home.

"Why in a home?" I asked, diverting her into the explanation that Albanian children had not had public schools in Kosovo since 1993. All public school classes were now conducted in Serbian and Albanian speakers had to create their own classrooms as best they could. The children of this family had been denied education by the Milosevic regime. I sat face to face with very early casualties of the war.

"Go on," I said.

Her teacher said to close their books and hurry home. She heard shooting as she ran along the narrow road to where she lived with her mother, two brothers and three sisters. Where was the father, I wondered but did not ask.

"What was your home like?" I asked.

A big house, she told me, surrounded by fields, a large garden, and quarters for their cow and seven chickens. Chickens and a cow. A peasant economy, more akin to the 1940's farm life I had known than to contemporary American life, I thought, discounting the three goats and five chickens in my own barn back home.

Awareness of the war had come gradually to Henkelinda. She heard about it first from newspapers, stories of fighting in Drenica, to the north, but the family and their neighbors went about their business as usual. It might happen to other people but not to us, they told themselves, much as Anna and Pere had in Vukovar.

Is that the same, I wondered, as the sure knowledge that I have, when I watch TV reports of distant wars, that they cannot touch me? Certainly not, I told myself, but even as this self-serving inner commentary silently accompanied Henkelinda's story, I sensed a growing lack of certainty.

Then, gradually, the families in their little settlement began to hear distant gunfire at night and could occasionally see the bursts of rockets exploding in the sky. Her mother kept the children away from the windows but the oldest boy, Nimi, liked the show and would sneak up to the attic to watch the fireworks. Downstairs the other kids would cry, afraid, as the windows rattled at each explosive burst.

"Were you afraid?" I asked.

She shook her head and laughed at such nonsense. No, she was not afraid for herself, but she did worry about her mother, who was already sick from high blood pressure. No, she was not afraid of the shooting and the bombs. But she was afraid of something else, she added softly – the soldiers. She had heard bad stories from her girlfriends and although she did not say the word (she probably didn't know it in English), I knew she was talking about rape. She was afraid to go to large towns, like Jacova, where the uniformed paramilitary roamed the streets in twos and threes. One day, in carrying a large empty pot to her uncle's house, she became terrified that they would stop her to see what was inside. A simple thing, to carry a pot down the street but she relived the feeling of that day, even as she spoke of it to me, much like I often relived my own search for the chain. Pot equals terror. Chain equals despair. She refused to go to Jacova after that although, I gathered because she lowered her voice as she told this story, she never told the others why. It was unlikely that her mother understood a single word of her daughter's story, yet she followed every movement of Henkelinda's mouth with her eyes.

Quickly things had gotten worse, there was no longer electricity at home and it was hard to find flour for the bread her mother baked each day. It fit my picture of their peasant life that the mother would make the daily bread.

One night she found her mother sitting in the darkened window looking at the sky, holding two-year old Gufim in her arms: "Oh moon," the older woman sobbed, what can we do, we hate this war." In the following days, each time Gufim saw the moon he'd paraphrase his mother's plea: "Oh moon, help us please."

Henkelinda stopped her story to translate to her mother, whose face softened into a smile that showed the gaps in her teeth.

Poor baby, I thought, as I looked to where Gufim hid behind his mother's large body, but his narrowed eyes were full of anger and his face was pinched with hate. The moon may have been his friend, but I was not.

"Was your father at home?" I asked.

"No," she said quickly and I pushed her to say more.

"Where is he now?" I asked.

"We do not know," she said, but I didn't believe her. He surely was a guerilla, member of the resistance army, the KLA, holed up in the mountains, fighting those vicious losing battles with the Serbian paramilitary, perhaps wounded, even dead. She must have imagined this as well but would not share such a painful suspicion with a stranger.

"How did you manage without him?" I asked.

"Mehmet, my mother's brother, helped us."

"Mehmet," echoed one of the little girls at our feet. I looked down and she who was Hita grinned broadly up at me. Henkelinda stroked her short hair. The older girl seemed more like mother than sister to these children and it was not just her command of English that made her stand out from the rest. In contrast to her mother's languor, her energy held the group together. Even Nare, younger by only one year, sat silently, dully, by her mother's side. But the upturned faces of the two girls sitting on the floor sparkled, as if Henkelinda was telling a happy story that they were able to follow, word for word. Maybe, for them, an American woman listening to it brightened those past troubles. A sense of responsibility weighed like lead on me. It was hard to breathe.

"We all love Mehmet very much," said Henkelinda, "Hita most of all."

She explained that their Uncle Mehmet lived in the town of Deçan (between Pec and Dakovica), while Henkelinda's family was in nearby Strelc a tiny cluster of houses to the north. I imagined a pioneer settlement out of Laura Ingalls Wilder, with two-room houses and chickens that came and went from yard to kitchen to yard. Much as the Rhode Island Red, Henny Penny, had wandered in through the squeaky screen door of my childhood kitchen to eat from the dog's dish.

I asked her to get back to June 30, 1998.

The bombardments were coming from every direction that day, and when she got home Mehmet was there, telling her family to come with him. She could see neighbors leaving their homes.

"What about the cow?" Dyke had asked.

"Forget the cow," her brother answered.

The valuable cow, I thought, but I was on the wrong track. The cow was a problem because of its nightly need to be milked, but they were more concerned about leaving the real valuables in their large stone home – two television sets, electrical appliances, a music center.

I had to revise my log cabin imaginings.

At Mehmet's house his family and mother joined them.

"Father refuses to leave, so we must go without him." Mehmet said to his sister, Dyke, and so 91-year old Hasan walked them to the gate, then turned and went back into the house.

I saw the old man clear as a bell – white hair, yellowing mustache, leaning on his cane. The spitting image of my Gramp, while the house he entered was surely the white clapboard farmhouse of my youth.

Henkelinda became less sure of herself at this point in her story. The intensity of her gaze into my eyes relaxed as she held impenetrable conversations with her family, tossed her hair and flashed me embarrassed smiles. Finally, with Dyke in tears, her daughter continued the story. I guessed that something had been left out.

That they were running away from threatening soldiers was clear. Less clear was what they were running toward. They traveled to small towns, some safer than others. The first day they went through the fields and woods to a place called Isniq, where they stayed four days before returning to Strelc where Mehmet, his family and their grandmother all stayed with them. Even in Strelc rockets rained down them each night from the nearby mountains, and although no one in the village was killed, some were wounded. As the firing extended into daylight hours, Mehmet decided they must leave again. Henkelinda remembered explosions, bombardments near them as they left.

Their first stop was a place called Lumbardh, where all the children were sick, the two oldest girls vomiting, everyone sleeping on hay, not daring to enter the houses, where soldiers made spot checks. Later they joined many others – at least 300 – in a wooded area, all sleeping under sheets of white plastic draped over sticks. Members of the KLA brought them supplies. One day a soldier led a cow into the camp, to provide milk for the babies, and men were always bringing flour for bread.

"We made 100 loaves of bread each day," said Henkelinda, shaking her hands in the air "I made too much bread – ow, how it hurt!"

There was the sound of gunfire, always, in the distance but as long as they were away from the houses, they were not attacked.

"Was anyone killed?" I asked.

"Many soldiers were killed and also one woman, by a stray bullet."

The KLA kept them moving, first to the village of Prapaqan, and when the Serbs came there, to Lumbardh, where they slept on the open ground. There was no food and Henkelinda's mother went begging for her sick children, asking local people for "just one egg." Henkelinda repeated in a comic voice "just one egg" in Albanian, producing giggles from the little girls and smiles from Dyke and Nare. Only little Gufim continued to frown.

One 3 AM the KLA woke them.

"Quickly to Kryshec. The Serbs are coming."

After two days the Serbs came to Kryshec and they moved to Isnic, where they hid for ten days by the river. And then . . .

"We had been going in a circle and after three weeks were back in Strelc."

The story was too much for me. I couldn't figure it out. Apparently the soldiers had been bent on chasing, not on killing. Where were they chasing these people to? I believed what this girl had told me, allowing for confusion of details. How could one cope, much less remember, when being hounded across the countryside in fear of their lives. What was this war about, anyway? Not that it mattered to me then. It was no longer politics, only the story of the little group with whom I sat. I wondered for a moment what I was doing there, how I had gotten in this place, and lifted the paper cup to my lips only to have a few grains of bitter grounds stick to my tongue. Henkelinda continued the story.

Their little settlement had been destroyed, the houses burned, their contents gone. The cows and chickens had disappeared. The Serb militia was gone but no one could live in Strelc anymore.

Mehmet left the others to return to Deçan, to see his father, but he found the house in ruins and the old man dead inside, his throat slit by the paramilitary. The storyteller stopped to converse with her mother, as if it was improper to tell such an important story in another language, without her parent's knowledge or consent. Dyke burst into tears but Henkelinda continued.

It was a terrible time for all the family, both Henkelinda's mother and grandmother became ill and Mehmet decided they must all go to Pristina, the capitol, where he said they would be safe.

"I didn't want to go," said Henkelinda. "Too many soldiers on the road."

But Mehmet had his way, and there were, as Henkelinda feared, Serbian militia everywhere. Escorted by twenty KLA, they left the roads and traveled through the fields and woods. In Klece, Mehmet made telephone calls, then sent them on to Lipljan where they hid again. Mehmet arranged the remainder of their trip to Pristina and that was the last time they saw him. He left to go to Albania, where his son already was.

As their father may have been, I imagined, wondering why she didn't mention it.

It took two weeks to get to Pristina, a distance of less than 40 miles, but there it was a different world.

"Pristina was wonderful. No fighting!"

The Red Cross gave them food and found them a house but after five weeks the owner asked them to leave.

"He needed it for his own relatives, who had been driven out of their village."

Eventually the family found themselves without money or a place to stay. The local mosque gave them 400 Deutschmark, roughly US$200. They began to listen to people who were talking about going to Bosnia.

"They said it was good in Sarajevo, lots of people were going there, and that the United Nations would take care of us and send us on to other European countries," said Henkelinda.

More than anything the family wanted to get back to Sweden where they had once lived – I didn't even try to understand when or why – and thought this might be the way, so they arranged to take a bus to Sarajevo along with Jecki, a young man betrothed to Nare, although she was only 15. Grandmother would stay behind in Pristina.

At the last minute, with the others already seated in the bus, it happened, her greatest fear – with her mother already seated on the bus, Henkelinda, doing a last minute errand, was hurrying down the street. It was there that she was stopped by police.

Her nightmare come true. "I was so afraid"

"Of what?"

"That they would not let me go."

"But why," I asked, "What had you done?"

"It was because I was from Deçan, they wanted to know why I had come to Pristina.

"Was that a crime?"

"They didn't like us, we were Albanian."

Stopped on the street by soldiers – what she had feared most for all those months – was happening, at this, the last moment before escape. But it was a nightmare and not reality, and they finally let her go to join her family. I wouldn't have known it turned out so well by the look on her face as she sat there. It took her a minute to start the story again.

The bus passed through two Serbian checkpoints, one out of Kosovo into Serbia proper, the second at the Bosnian border. Jecki and other young men left the bus before each border post, cut through the woods and were picked up beyond. Being of military age, they would have been taken away, forced into the Serbian army, or worse. At the border everyone got out of the bus and was searched by the guards, who took all their papers, passports and money. The guards said they must pay 500 DM.

"I said we had no money, said Henkelinda, "but a woman guard searched me and found the 400 DM. I shouted at her that it was all we had but she didn't care and took it anyway." She laughed as she said it and grabbed at the pocket of her jeans as she must have done before the guard. This girl had major spunk!

They arrived in Sarajevo and right away discovered that it was not true that the United Nations would help them go to other European countries. That first night they were given bread and marmalade by a United Nations worker ("Marmalade!" said Henkelinda, "Ugh!" and I felt a pang for poor Godsticker) and three cots for the family. Gufim and Dyke were sick that first night. After several days, on September 20, they were taken to Hadžići, this United Nations refugee camp where we were sitting.

"In Coca-Cola oh my god, how many people!" Henkelinda waved her arms about, to encompass 1200 of her countrymen, most of them, including Jecki, living on the open factory floors. The seven-member family got one of the fifteen canvas tents.

Well, there it was. This was the story I heard, sitting maybe half an hour on that hard bench. I lifted the cup to my lips and my tongue grazed the clump of cold grounds stuck to the bottom. I had no idea where Mary was and less what I would do next. What I was in – the middle of six children and a weak helpless woman – was so big it overwhelmed me. I had no ways to deal – words to say – things to feel – about what I had heard. It wasn't a story, a book, a TV drama. I couldn't close the pages, turn off the set. It was happening to me.

No, not the things that had happened to these people – something else. I was discovering the unbelievably uncomfortable truth that the only thing that separated me from them other than language, was circumstance, and what circumstance! I saw it all, how this family had been living their lives in familiar ways: two teenagers who listened to music and watched TV, two young girls who played soccer and did homework, a bratty toddler who clung to his mom, a boy – well, I hadn't met Nimi yet. Then came the war and that world was turned upside down.

When I had first walked into that tent they were different; REFUGEE was written across their chests, making them a different species, with different expectations, deserving a different fate, to be pitied and helped perhaps, in ways that were not disruptive to the helper. I'd thought I was doing them a favor by sitting down and drinking their coffee, which could not have been easy for Nare to make. That thought was gone. They had the same entitlements as me; to turn it around, they were no more deserving of life in this tent than I was. Whatever was I going to do with that? I was going to have to do something, I knew. But what?

That's the way I saw it later, after my thoughts had caught up with my feelings, after I had talked to Mary, had returned the next day to the camp and spent many more hours with Henkelinda.

All I felt at that particular moment, the story being over, as I stood up and disgracefully fished that 20 DM note out of my wallet, was a closing down inside, a wanting to lock up my brain, to take a nap, to go to sleep, above all to get away as far and as fast as I could.

All I could say was "I must go to find my friend."

CHAPTER 5

ME OR THEM

"I won't forget you," had been my promise to Henkelinda. As if I had a choice. Back in the states I thought of little else and set about what I am good at – asking questions. I called and e-mailed United Nations workers in Bosnia, in Germany, in New York, looking for ways to get Henkelinda and her family out of the camp.

"How can I help?" I asked.

"Send gifts," one bureaucrat said, as if socks and sweaters could balance the hideously lopsided scales between Henkelinda's life and mine.

"Don't promise anything you can't deliver," a young staffer lectured me.

"Don't get involved," each cautioned, as if involvement were an ugly thing. Wasn't involvement what the world needed more of? Wasn't involvement what Bosnia had needed before, when we had delivered too little much too late? And it was clear to me now that western governments would be no more effective in preventing a Kosovar disaster than they had been in Bosnia.

Shortly after Mary and I returned home, Richard Holbrooke announced an agreement with Milosevic that satisfied NATO's conditions for withdrawing the threat to bomb. This new postponement was indefinite, tied to Milosevic's promise to withdraw troops, cease hostilities, and all the rest. To insure that those promises were being kept, representatives from the Organization for Security and Cooperation in Europe (OSCE) would monitor on the ground, NATO airplanes from the sky. The diplomats trooped off to Belgrade to sign new agreements, effective October 25. Wrangling continued, over which troops would be withdrawn, how many and how fast, but by the following day there were signs the Yugoslavian troops were moving, which responsible diplomats such as Solana, Clark and Holbrooke had to acknowledge as progress, the kind of progress that is better than a war. And not to be outdone, the UN passed a third resolution, 1203, to show that it approved of all these new developments. I discounted all this diplomatic hard work because I had lost interest in it. All I wanted was to help my new friends.

The thought came to me, in mid-November – what I must do, if do I must. I must go back.

My children were spending Christmas with their in-laws – as they did every other year – and my own holiday plans were vague. I would return to Hadžići and maybe, together with Henkelinda and her family, we could find a way for me to really help.

This thought did not simply come to me in gentle ways, slipping into my mind through normal channels. It took a devious untested route, barreling and blasting into my brain where it exploded into a thousand motes of fine white dust that settled over every cell – a thought that would have been, before, unthinkable. Go back to Sarajevo, go to spend Christmas with a family I had met but twice, the very act of going a commitment in itself, commitment to do what I had never done before, had no idea how to do, had no reason to expect success from. It was, perhaps, a mental deviation, a "seizure" of sorts, a short circuiting, back firing, fuse-blowing surge of electrical impulses, an excessive stimulation of the temporal lobe. Where had it come from? Not from anything I knew. Go back to Sarajevo? For god sakes why?

That, my own question, was echoed by everyone I knew. I had a life, a family, why was I stepping so far out, so far away? One fear was that my own children, at least if they knew how strong and deep this thing was in my heart, would feel hurt for being left outside. Another fear was that I would look to be the goodie-two-shoes lady that I was, of course, quite sure I actually was. Among the arguments that I got from both myself and others were:

"Why help one family, when there are so many?"

"What arrogance, to think that you can make a difference!"

"It may make you feel good, but it won't do anything for them!"

That was the risk. To go would definitely make me feel good – at least less bad – but if it didn't change their lives, it was no more useful than the 20 DM note or a backpack of cheap books and toys.

Bronchial flu hit me in mid-December and the fever made me despair of doing anything, much less helping this family improve their lives; I almost gave up the plan to go. But as my temperature fell, my spirits rose and on Christmas Eve afternoon I flew into Sarajevo, alone. Alone in December felt very different, as the plane settled on the snow-banked runway, from October, with Mary. Colder, emptier, less friendly, closer to wartime than recovery.

Dirt-encrusted snow piled high along the road from the airport, sidewalks were empty and doors were shut tight against the bitter cold.

I climbed a dark staircase to my high ceilinged cubbyhole room in the Hotel Dardanija. Downstairs behind the desk Fatima told me in her sparse English that I was their only guest. She locked the door when I went out to find a restaurant and said to ring the bell when I returned.

I stayed off the icy sidewalks and walked in the crunch and slush of the street along the river to the Slovenian Club. The hills beyond the river which once sparkled with rifle and mortar fire were sparsely spangled with the tiny lights of homes. Cars crept along the snowy streets. I passed one man and then a couple, heads tucked down and faces hidden in scarves. The temperature was in the single digits Fahrenheit and the air crackled.

Stairs led from the sidewalk down to the restaurant, a hot little room where two waiters scurried among the tables and the wide-girthed owner barked out orders from where he lounged behind the bar. I sat near a table of five American soldiers – members of SFOR, the United Nations peacekeeping force – one woman, one black and three white men. They spoke to one another formally, as strangers do, as homesick servicemen forced to eat together in feigned Christmas Eve congeniality might do. My own distance from home felt to be much further than theirs, which was itself far shorter than my distance from them. I could not speak to them, identify myself as being from that place in the universe that was their home and mine, because I would have had to explain why I wasn't where I could have by choice been, a choice that was not theirs. There was no sense, no reality, to my being in this place. I could have been a visitor from the moon. I could not have explained why I was there. I certainly didn't know myself, as I went through the motions of ordering a bowl of soup, a veal chop and a glass of white wine turned bitter in my mouth from the antibiotics coursing through my veins. I was outside and looking in, above and looking down.

A blast of cold wind struck my back as a man burst through the door, hugging a mass of red roses to his chest, offering them to the room to buy. A customer came forward from the back but when he heard the cost he rubbed his fingers together in the universal gesture meaning "pricey" and went back to his table empty handed.

Sarajevo roses – it seemed appropriate that they would come so dear, and when the restaurant owner stepped forward to buy two, offering one to me, the other to the female soldier, the gratitude and sorrow that welled up in my heart anchored me again in my body, in the world. I became as real here as I might have been at home, as the soldiers were, the waiters . . .the generous gesture brought me back to life, caught my being up with my body. I tucked the rose deep inside my coat as I hurried back to the hotel and set it askew in a glass of water carefully balanced on the little T.V. Such a simple thing, it had transformed my world. I snuggled deep into my bed, intensely happy to be where I was, excited for the coming day.

The empty tram I took on Christmas Day was unheated, its windows frosted over and the floor filthy with winter puddles, but I scarcely noticed, buoyed by the intense excitement of coming closer at each click of the wheels on the track to the family that were now for me mounted on that fantasy pedestal of where I would join them, lifting them above the squalor of their undeserved circumstance. I even thought of staying with them that night in the tent, a way of saying we are the same and only an accident of time and place has made you, and not me, a refugee. I thought, believed that I could do it, with all my heart.

"Coca Cola," I told the taxi driver when I left the streetcar at the end of its line. He spoke no English but was sure to know the location of the former bottling plant so recently transformed into a refugee camp. I left the taxi waiting at the gate, thinking they might have moved elsewhere, by now. I had had no way of telling them I was coming, and the UNHCR had promised, in October, to place them in better, warmer, quarters before it got too cold. It now qualified as *too cold*, certainly.

Two months before, hundreds of pairs of eyes had watched Mary and me cross the yard that separated the gate from the living quarters, but today the cold had driven most residents indoors. Painted in shades of dreary grey, it was an unfamiliar place, a no man's land. The cold had drained the color, the life, the reality from my memories, stifled any odors from the line of porta potties. This place had lost its meaning in my life, was Kafka's castle, a nightmarish nowhere.

In the center of this vast landscape of nothingness a small bundled group was gathered, far down the line of tents. Too far to recognize the faces yet, as one turned toward me, I knew it to be Henkelinda as surely as she knew the long black-coated stranger to be me. Dream came to life and as she waved and shouted, I did too and in an instant Henkelinda was running toward me, materializing at my side as miraculously as that first time 60 days before. But this time she flung her arms around me.

"I knew you'd come back," she said.

How could she have known. I didn't.

Moments later Esad came up from behind, his great gummy smile filling his handsome face. I had found what I had come for, and I hugged and held them close. We moved slowly toward the tent where I had sat and sipped Albanian coffee and bursting in to where the family sat clustered tightly together, we began the talk which filtered from my English through Esad's good understanding and Henkelinda's partial one into Albanian for the others, where ideas and thoughts flowed back and forth with an ease that belied the awkwardness of the words.

"How is it here, now?" I asked. The answers were not good.

The mother had waked, that morning, with ice in her hair. Temperatures in the tent had been below freezing each night for a week. We sat close by a metal stove that 12-year old Nimi fed continually with small pieces of freshly splintered wood. I had on an ankle-length sheepskin coat, a fur lined hood and a scarf, but my toes quickly turned numb and my nose ran constantly. The others were only in jackets and sweaters and Nare had no socks. The stove had been hot enough, however, to burn Gufim when he rushed against it earlier that week. Wrapped in gauze from fingers to elbow, he whined endlessly, spit at his sisters and eyed me even more sullenly, if that was possible, than before. It was Christmas day, for me. For them it was Ramadan and we would not go to a restaurant until 4:15, after the sun had set. It was ten in the morning and it would be a long day. Somewhere in the camp the morning allotment of food had arrived, and Hita and Nika sat cross-legged on the wooden floor, dipping pieces torn from a loaf of bread into bowls of stew. They were too young to observe the Muslim sunrise-to-sunset fast.

Their biggest news was a chance to move to more permanent, warmer quarters nearby. The promise had been made, the things were packed and piled behind us on the beds, but it hadn't happened. The mother didn't want to go.

"How do I know it's better?" she asked.

"Wouldn't anything be better?" I asked her back. She sighed. She knew better than I that there could always be worse than even very bad. I reminded myself of her weeks of travel through the woods, the children with her, escaping the town where her house, her life, her father had been destroyed. I could not imagine how this slack-bodied, sad-eyed woman had managed it. I remembered then the taxi I had left waiting outside the camp, not being sure I'd find my friends inside.

"Let's go see the new place," I said.

"It's too far to walk," said Henkelinda.

"But not too far to ride," I said triumphantly.

And so Esad, Henkelinda and I were off, a short stretch down the main asphalted road and then a long slow rollicking trip along the frozen rutted freshly-bulldozed dirt road to the new camp.

"I must stop here," the driver finally said, but promised to wait once more. Business paid for out of an American purse was not easily come by in Ilidza.

We climbed the hill to the low narrow building of pine boards to inspect the barren rows of cubbyholes that stretched along the long dark corridor. Smelling of fresh-cut wood, each tiny door-less room had two bunk beds, three feet apart. Henkelinda looked around unhappily.

"Mama won't like it." she said, "There is no privacy."

The seven of them would be separated, spread out among two or even three such cubbyholes, but there was a hanging electric bulb, a space heater and a window in each compartment, all lacking in the tent. Each barrack housed sixty people and there were toilet stalls and sinks at one end of the building, stoves and tables for eating at the other. It was a vast improvement over Hadžići, if one did not mind communal living.

We went next to the occupied building, next door, where camp residents had already moved in. The community room was filled to overflowing with women and small children. Henkelinda gurgled with pleasure to see former friends and was sucked into conversations. Esad led me over to an old man seated by himself.

"He knows you're an American and he wants to talk to you. I'll translate."

Red-eyed, his chin covered with stubble, mouth full of broken teeth, the man spoke in rasping, angry tones.

"Kosovo must be independent from Serbia," Esad was translating loosely, tidying up the emotional torrent of words, "and we will fight for it. I'm going back to join the army myself." He paused. His hands were shaking.

"Tell everyone that we will fight – that we will fight to the death. Even if we all die, we will fight. Every one of us." He was exhausted and his attention drifted off.

I didn't want to hear those things. From all reports delivered to my hotel room that morning by CNN, the Albanians remaining in Kosovo, vastly out manned and ill equipped, were being slaughtered by the powerful Serbian army. Unless outside armies joined them, any fight would be inevitably to the death. I looked around the room and guessed that he did not speak for everyone. Mothers of small children do not talk about fighting to the death.

"Let's go," I muttered to Esad. We found Henkelinda and left.

Back in the tent with Henkelinda's full report, the mother sighed again. This time it was "What shall I do?" a sigh well understood in every language.

"Move," we all urged and so she agreed to do, the following afternoon.

Esad, the new camp's English teacher

The hours of this day were passing slowly. Esad left to teach at the school, staffed entirely by camp residents, and five of us tagged after him. Hita, Nika and Nimi joined the other children on the floor mats, all wearing heavy coats. Henkelinda and I sat to the side. There was no longer feeling in my toes and uselessly I rubbed away at them. Esad was teaching English and the lesson was on body parts. He drew an ugly misshapen head on the board and asked the children if he had forgotten anything.

"Snot," cried out one kid, and Esad dribbled mucous from each nostril.

"Nits," shouted another, and he attached tiny dots of chalk on the stiffly upright strands of hair.

"What shall we call this guy," he asked the children. It was unanimous: "Leonardo Di Caprio!" No matinee-idol worshipers here. If they must suffer those indignities, then so must the universally-admired star of The Titanic.

They settled down and learned their lesson well, jumping up to recite individually and shouting responses in noisy unison. They ended by reviewing how to introduce themselves in English and when Esad asked them to practice on each other – "hello, how are you, I am fine, what is your name?" several came over to partner with me.

When class was over, at least for Henkelinda, Esad and me – the children moved on to mathematics – the sun had sunk toward the pines along the ridge behind the camp but still had a stretch of blue sky to cover before it would disappear. I pondered whether my bladder would hold out until then and decided, no. Henkelinda insisted on checking out the outdoor toilets first, leading me to one presumably less soiled than the others. That which had been deposited upon the floor instead of down the hole, however, was happily frozen solid. We went back to the tent.

By the time the sun had finally slipped behind the pines young Gufim was throwing himself about with angry sobs and Mama opted for the two of them to stay behind. The rest of us broke free of the camp, Nimi, Hita and Nika running past the trailer-office, whose occupants took no heed of the comings and goings, through the gate and onto the road to town, bright with the lights of evening traffic.

"They'll surely get run over before the bus arrives," I said to Esad, and he laughed. It was an inappropriate American anxiety, not fitting for these kids, who had faced and overcome real dangers. I walked at only a slightly slower pace with Esad, Nare and her boyfriend Jecki, and Henkelinda with her arm clinging tightly to mine. A van pulled out from the gloom behind us and Esad waved it down.

"Room for six more?"

"Why not?" the driver said and although it was already filled to overflowing, we managed to squeeze in, sitting three-deep in the back.

Running, skipping, laughing, shouting, the little ones made their way through the snow to the Ilidza restaurant of their choice – the Pizzeria Diablo. We burst into the too-hot mostly empty room and ordered in noisy confusion, with Esad translating into Bosnian for the waiter. It was a glorious meal. Although the pizza, by Chicago standards, was abominable, Nimi and Esad cleaned up two platters worth. Henkelinda, teasing Esad and sassing her brother and sisters, worked her way through a mountain of spaghetti. Little Nika and Hita giggled a lot, shared my opinion of the pizza, but slurped up large and whipped-cream laden desserts. A giant hamburger was ordered to take back to Mama.

"What I like best is meat, pizza and coca cola," Esad declared," and I have them all, so I am a happy man."

Christmas dinner at Pizzaria Diablo

The waiter handed out balloons which, with magic markers, the others decorated with symbols of the KLA. Esad gave me an illustrated history lesson on their homeland's not-so-glorious recent past. Everyone used the toilets.

The waiter took Esad aside and asked, "Who is that woman?"

"She's taking us all to America tomorrow," Esad joked.

"Tell her to take me too!"

Most legal ways to travel in the world are closed to refugees. I would have taken them all to America in a minute, if it were possible, and had fruitlessly explored other possible ways to be of help. All I could do, for now, was buy a pizza pie and yet it felt to me, with all the love and laughter at the table that night, as good as any Christmas dinner can get. They were so full of life, so beautiful, I felt so wonderfully good – good about them, about how the day had worked out, and very good about myself.

Shards of icy air shot up my arms and down my neck as we jostled each other through the door into the black night. The children floundered over the snowdrifts onto the wide parking lot where buses to Hadžići hunkered down in the bitter cold. At the front of the line, giving off impatient puffs of exhaust, theirs was ready to go. Waving back at me over their heads, they clambered up the steps. The doors slammed shut and I stood there alone, feeling an unbearable ache of cold rising from the ground up through my feet. I hurried across the lot to where the lights from two tram cars shone dimly through the ice and dirt encrusted windows.

I was the only passenger back to Sarajevo, as the train rattled and squealed at snail's pace, stopping at each street light. More cold worked its way from the metal seat up through my spine and into my brain. All thoughts of the Christmas pizza dinner had disappeared, as well as of its participants. All I could think about was how unbelievably cold I was. I raged at being in that place when there were other places to be, angry at myself for the stupid choices that caused myself this much pain, hating this train ride of such misery. I didn't dare move – the slightest motion sent cold shocks deeper into my bones. Frozen remnants of my mind tracked the tram's progress – ah, we're passing the Holiday Inn, here's the branch off to the right, two more blocks, just past this light if it ever turns green, now I can stand up and pull the cord. Yes, slowing down, door opening, one step, a second, onto the lumpy piles of ice. Oh God, I can move now, if my body, which I could no longer feel, still works. Across the street, half running in the snow – the sidewalk glaze is too treacherous – the hotel's light is just beyond those trees, I'm almost there. Almost there. Almost there. Behind me a muffled blast rose from high up in the hills, surely a land mine, set off by – what? – who cares?! It wasn't my god damn country, no one I knew was up there, above all, nor was I. And then I was opening the hotel door, hit by a rush of hot air, yes, it was over. And in the instant, knowing that I would now be warm again, the pain dropped away, the anger in my head dissolved.

Upstairs, tearing off the coat, scarf, gloves, socks, stockings, sweater, slacks, throwing them on the floor, I crawled under the blanket in my underwear and held my breath, listening to the steam sputtering from the red hot radiator, each piece of me beginning to warm. There was no frostbite, no medical emergency, no trauma or crisis of any kind. I had simply been very, very cold. As my brain cells began to thaw and function but before they'd wrapped themselves in their normal protective shields, they let slip a single thought that turned my idea of myself, nanoseconds later, upside down – *I'm glad it's me that's warm in here* was what I thought. It wasn't a prayer of gratitude or even a twinge of guilt, it was a statement of personal values – the emphasis had been on the *me*. If in this world there are those that are warm and those that are cold, this thought expressed, I want it to be me that's in the former group. And I could hear the ugly underside of that thought – *and that it's someone else, in this case **them**, that are in the other group.*

On that Christmas day I had almost convinced myself that I was a really good person – coming back to this place, spending the day with them, the pizza, the promise to help, the sitting around in that god awful freezing tent, and then it had slipped out. If I was ever put to the test – them or me, me or them – I'd opt for me. I couldn't even handle a little cold. I wasn't such a good person after all. The cat was out of the bag. I was going to have to live with that. So be it. Being warm and comfortable, I slept.

Self-examination gave way to the business at hand, the next morning, when Henkelinda, Esad and Jecki arrived at the hotel – Dyke would not allow Henkelinda to travel unaccompanied with Esad, a single man, and the presence of Nare's fiancee made it, in her eyes if not mine, okay. With his slouch, his slicked back hair and guarded ways of always watching me, I did not see him as a member of the family that I loved. When I came downstairs Fatima was in deep conversation with the three of them. Clearly she was baffled by my presence in the city, much less my motley assortment of guests.

I had done my homework and we four proceeded to make the rounds of agencies and embassies in Sarajevo, collecting information and papers that might lead to their escape from the Coca Cola camp. There was no possibility of normal migration to another country, even a temporary one. While Esad and Jecki had both escaped from Kosovo with current Serbian passports, as they circled away from and around the border guards, Dyke and her children had none. The international legal status of those seven people was that of *refugee* and countries have very specific policies regarding such. Ann Sides had left the American consulate but I was told emphatically by others there that there was no channel for a refugee to get to America, a country that makes cautious and conservative policy determinations as to what countries' residents it will accept. So much for letting the world's poor and huddled masses through our gates! While the road to America was completely blocked, the route to Western Europe was full of red tape. Sweden was one of the few countries that was accepting Kosovar Albanians, and at the Swedish embassy, a mass of people pressed toward the window where a young woman doled out information in four languages. Henkelinda and Esad made requests to her in pleading tones, which she abruptly dismissed. As they were about to turn away I pushed past them and in English angrily demanded the applications that had been denied.

"We will be the judge of whether they qualify," I snapped. She pushed the forms across the counter.

"I could not have spoken to her like that," Henkelinda said, on the street outside.

"It's easy to be tough when you carry an American passport," I said and that's exactly what it was. We Americans take for granted and are accorded privileges, wherever we go in the world, that are hard for others to come by. We have our own sense of entitlement. Even this hybrid language of ours reaps unearned respect.

We pushed into a steamy café for a coffee – Esad had a Coke – and shuffled through the Swedish documents. There were some major roadblocks, the biggest of which was the requirement for a Swedish sponsor. Henkelinda actually knew a family there, a kindly couple who sent them socks and warm sweaters in the mail, perhaps a possible sponsor. Henkelinda would produce their phone number for a call from my hotel, the following day. I offered up money to the waiter, adding a few shilling as a tip. Jecki grabbed my hand.

"No."

"What?" I turned to Esad.

"He says you pay too much, the waiter is gypping you."

"No, I'm giving him the extra of my own free will."

It was not a familiar concept nor one that Jecki approved of, his frown suggested.

There was one more stop to make that day – a bank. I knew their way out of the country would cost me money, and once I left Bosnia I'd need a way of sending it. My plan was to open a joint account in the names of Jecki and Esad – a passport was required – so that I could wire what was necessary. I explained our intent at an impressive looking bank on Tito Blvd. The woman at the teller's window looked confused. I started to explain in more detail.

"No, no," she said, it's not that. It's just that . . . well . . . tomorrow we will close our doors."

"Close your doors?"

"I'm not supposed to say it. We will close down. We have no more money."

"Oh." Sarajevo was not an easy place.

We went to another bank where, if they were closing tomorrow, no one was letting on. Esad and Jecki signed the necessary papers, I produced ten Deutschmarks to open the account and recorded the account number in my notebook. I didn't know if this would work, if it would ever have to work, but it seemed to me a necessary step. The young people made no comment on the transaction, thinking perhaps that I knew what I was doing and that it made sense.

By the time we had made the phone call to Sweden, the following day, having followed up with a few more dead end visits to government offices, the situation looked bleak. I explained the family's predicament to the woman who answered the phone and whose English was good enough. She excused herself for several minutes and her husband came on.

"What is meant by this sponsorship?" he asked.

I knew what he wanted to know. Would it cost them money and if so, how much. I didn't know the answer.

"If there are costs, I will be glad to help," I said.

"No, we cannot do this thing," he said and hung up.

On the day before I was to leave, I sat with the family and Esad in their new quarters. Heavy gray blankets were hung for privacy but it was hard to talk above the corridor hubbub and heads popped uninvited through the flap. The heat was stifling. Dyke lay on a lower bunk, her head half out the open window. Nare stretched out silently above her while Jecki stood nearby, slouched and smoking, suspicious of the words he could not understand. The young ones ran noisily in and out. We went over the papers and information we had gathered, both languages rumbling about in endless translation. The meaning became clear.

"There's no way," I said. Words of despair, both theirs and mine.

Jecki half turned from me to talk in Albanian, both to Nare and to the room.

"There is a way," Henkelinda said to me, "Jecki knows a man who would get us out if we paid him."

It was no secret that people were smuggled out, here as elsewhere in the world where living conditions were less tolerable than risk of death. Wherever people were willing to take that risk, others were willing to promise them to help, promises they could or would only sometimes keep.

"That's too dangerous," I snapped, thinking of suffocated Chinese and drowned Cubans who had tried this underground route to a better life.

We argued back and forth, but in the end the choices were clear. They could stay in this awful place for who knew how long – the Serbians had pummeled the Bosnians four years before the western powers stepped in to help – or make a run for it. They could not do the latter without my help but I'd already made the decision so my words came easily.

"If you're willing to take that risk, I'll find the money."

I didn't want to – need to – know the cost. Henkelinda translated and they all, even Dyke, beamed.

"We will do it," said Henkelinda.

I never believed that six children and an exhausted mother could or would negotiate the traps and terrors of illegally crossing hostile international borders. I underestimated my Henkelinda.

CHAPTER 6

THE LONGEST SPRING

JAN 1 TO FEB 9

Henkelinda called two weeks later to say they had negotiated a price with the flesh-smugglers who promised them escape to Western Europe. It was Esad, by her side, who did the talking – without her hands and eyes as backup, her English fell apart. For $18,000 all nine – the six Asanaj children and their mother, Jecki and Esad – would be given false Croatian passports and taken to Stuttgart, Germany. They'd be there, they were told, in no more than five days.

The next step was mine, but the decision, the hard part, had been made in that overheated cubicle outside Sarajevo. Only the execution, far easier, remained, although it would require resources greater than my own. I called a friend who called a friend and by the miracle of wired transfers – the money seemed to pass through all the banks of Europe before it reached the one in Sarajevo – on February 9, they called to say they had the eighteen thousand in their hands. I was elated; the deal was as good as done. Or so I thought.

They could, of course, take the money and exit my world. Even as we had sat together in December and I made the commitment, I understood that risk. It didn't worry me. I thought I knew what they wanted, who they were and how they would behave. It was an act of gambler's faith.

They had no reasonable choice other than this illegal emigration. The conditions in the dead-end Bosnian refugee camp were intolerable for any length of time and going home looked less likely every day. The Western organizations had been scurrying about to implement their side of the October agreements. The OSCE was busy recruiting and flying observers into Kosovo, but by the end of December there were only 400 of the promised 2000 on the ground, only 11 of which were part of their important Human Rights Division, the folks that would do the job of documenting violations of the eight international agreements that Yugoslavia had signed over the years. NATO was even busier, not only in the sky setting up the aerial surveillance mission but also in Macedonia, where a French-led 2000-man task force had been established to pull the OSCE folks out in case of war. Just in case.

All this energy was expended to confirm what most people already knew – that Serb attacks on Albanian civilians, using tanks and armored vehicles, were continuing, as the KLA was ratcheting up the stakes. Each time a masked Serbian squadron stormed an Albanian village to drag a man from his bed or kidnap him off the streets, another man – or two, or ten – would join the rebel group. Terror and terrorism reigned on both sides, just beyond the OSCE's line of sight.

What apparently happened in Racaq on January 15 should have been no surprise. Once a village of 2,000, only 400 people were living there when masked Serbs in a brutal pre-dawn assault, murdered 45 civilians including 23 men who were marched out of town and executed. There was rumored to be a KLA base in town, but the indiscriminate shooting at family members as they ran from their beds was a hallmark of paramilitary butchery. The Racaq massacre triggered a protest by William Walker, the OSCE head and a demand by Louise Arbour, chief prosecutor at the ICTY, to be allowed to investigate. Milosevic stonewalled, refusing Arbour an entry visa and threatening to throw Walker out of the country. NATO's Solana issued a statement of protest, on January 28, that the October agreements had been violated – arbitrary detentions, mutilation of unarmed civilians, extra-judicial killings were being documented by the OSCE, but instead of initiating the military solution that had been threatened three months before, dumped the problem into the soft and squishy lap of the Contact Group for a diplomatic solution.

The Contact Group, which was comprised of the United States, Britain, France, Germany and Russia and had been so impotent during the early 90's while the Serbs set about destroying the other Yugoslavian states, proposed the classic international response to military bullying – a conference, this one to be held on February 6 in Rambouillet, France. Their official January 29 statement pompously summoned the warring parties – the Albanians and the Serbs – to the French city, *demanding* that they successfully negotiate the Kosovar issues in seven days and reach a political settlement within three weeks. It meant that NATO, the only organization that I thought could stop Milosevic, had stepped aside.

That's it, I thought, I've got to get those people OUT!

I was feeling good. Amid all this diplomatic stalling I was saving lives. I was extending the chain to bring a family out of the cesspool of refugee camp life in Bosnia into the western European land of plenty. I was feeling so good, in fact, that on February 8 I quit my job. I had dreamed of doing just that for months (and even years), making a break away from my only source of income to what I had wanted for half a century – a full time writing life. Although I had done much of my environmental consulting out of my home, a bi-weekly commute to Chicago and the daily intrusion of telephone calls, faxes, internet research and writing made attention to the book I had been working on for almost a year a slapdash thing. I imagined that it was external circumstance that held me back, that if I could sweep everything else off my desk, I'd settle down to what should have been – could still be – my life's work. After six decades of cautious navigating, I was finally going to take the leap. If I could save lives I could do anything. I was on a high risk roll.

In a second hazardous leap I started to take Prozac. Another premeditated step, I'd been playing with the idea since the anti-depression drug first hit the market and the press. It was, among some of my friends and associates, a minor rage. *It lets you be yourself*, they told me, a stronger and more focused self. That was for me! I didn't see myself as depressed, just not quite up to snuff. I had these late afternoon downers when I had the energy of a snail. The new me couldn't tolerate this downtime, the new me was writing books and saving lives. I found a shrink who decided, after one brief interview, that I was the perfect candidate for the anti-depressant. On February 5 I took my first pill and waited for the sky to open up.

All this left me spinning like a top. When I laid my head down on the pillow, each night, racing thoughts kept me awake, and when I woke before dawn I'd hustle through my early routine – to feed my darling Portuguese Water Dog, Bête Noire, toss birdseed onto the deck, make coffee and settle in my reading chair – excited for the promise of the day. But as I let the caffeine perform its miracle, dog snuggled close by, and as I planned out my daily writing schedule, I battled a disturbing whirlwind of thoughts centered on Henkelinda and her family. I was counting on the Prozac to help.

FEB 10 TO MARCH 21

I was also waiting for the telephone to ring. The few times that I tried to call the camp, asking for Esad, voices barked out *Ne,* but I had no idea what *No* meant – that he was no longer there, couldn't come to the phone, or didn't want to talk to me? After four nerve-racking weeks, on March 11, Henkelinda and Esad telephoned to say the family would leave the next day. That was the good news. The bad news was that Esad would not go. His 17-year old brother had recently arrived in the camp, escaped from their Mitrovica home where the Serbs were making regular forays in search of men of military age, and his mother had moved the family into the woods above their home. She was afraid and sent him to be with his older brother in the Bosnian camp. Esad gave me the number of an American missionary in Ilidza whom he sometimes visited and where messages could be left.

"What shall I do with my share of the money?" he asked.

"Put it in the bank. You will need it someday," I said.

"Five days to Germany," Henkelinda told me, bubbling through the crackling line as they signed off, "five days!"

Five days went by and I heard nothing more. Then five more. I took a snapshot taken in Hadžići in October, cropped out Henkelinda's face, enlarged it to fit a 8 x 10 frame and propped it before my reading chair where each morning, with my pre-dawn cup of coffee, I looked at her and she at me.

"Where are you now?" I asked with only Bête to hear, a ritual to keep her alive for me.

As Sarajevo gradually receded into memory, I begin to realize that I had set something in motion that was turning the lives of eight people upside down. What I had called excitement transformed into anxiety. After all, the refugee camp, with all its miseries, had been safe. Illegally crossing hostile borders at the mercy of traffickers in human cargo was not. If something went wrong I, by making it possible, would be responsible. The creeping suspicion that things could go, perhaps already had gone, wrong churned my stomach night and day.

Meanwhile, the outcome of more than two weeks of talks at Rambouillet confirmed my earlier misgivings. The two parties to the Kosovar conflict, surrounded by Contact Group dignitaries and their staffs, refused to sign the voluminous Chapters of the Agreement prepared by the non-combatants. The Europeans and Americans satisfied themselves, when the conference broke up on February 23, by endorsing the document themselves and scheduling another meeting on March 15. More diplomats got back into the act – Senator Bob Dole went to Macedonia to meet with Kosovar Albanians and Richard Holbrooke went to Belgrade to meet with Milosevic.

A second meeting did occur, in the Kleber Center in Paris, from March 15 to 18. The Albanians surprised everyone by finally agreeing to sign the document, and Belgrade surprised no one by refusing. While everyone else was focused on the words of Rambouillet, Milosevich had taken action on the ground. By the time the meetings broke up, one third of his armed forces were massed in and around Kosovo. They began a new initiative, driving hundreds of Kosovar Albanians out of their homes and onto the roads, generating scattered fighting throughout the province and harassing the international monitors. On March 20 the OSCE hastily departed and as they did, all hell broke loose.

Serb forces surged into and across the western section of Kosovo in a massive ethnic cleansing that left burning houses and dead bodies in its wake. Another Sarajevo, worse yet, another Srebrenica, appeared to be in the making. At least Henkelinda and her family were on their way to safety. Or so I hoped.

On March 21 I got a call from Henkelinda. Not from Germany but from Zagreb, a stone's throw from Sarajevo. After ten days they had not yet left the Balkans.

"What are you doing there?" I shouted into the phone, but her English had fallen apart.

"Refugee camp," I understood, but little else along the noisy line.

But they had at least made it through one danger zone – the Serbian part of Bosnia where, had they been caught, they would have been sent back, imprisoned or worse. Zagreb was the capital of Croatia, and they had Croatian passports. Surely things would be okay. I said as much.

"No passports." said Henkelinda, "Police send us to Ljubljana."

"Police? Ljubljana?" The phone went dead.

Where was Ljubljana, I wondered, and dragging out my atlas, found it to be the capital of Slovenia. They were inching toward the Italian border where they expected to escape the former Yugoslavia, but now I wondered if they'd ever make it through. Why were they dealing with the police and what had happened to the promised passports? It sunk in slowly but when it did I felt the fool – they had been duped by the guys that took their money. Of course, it happened all the time! What had I been thinking! But I had no idea what to do about it. I was way over my head and could only sit and wait.

I wasn't very good at that. Whatever Prozac provided, it was not inner peace. I was a mass of nerves. I couldn't sleep, my hand shook perceptibly as I lifted the early morning cup of coffee, and my mind began to leave my body in disturbing ways. During one pre-dawn review of notes I'd taken during a stay in Bangkok, I drifted off and my mind revisited that Asian city. I came back to Indiana with a start – focus was fine but out-of-body travel wasn't. I was even more unnerved as I started off in my Honda Civic the next morning, listening to the radio news. At the end of my driveway, I stopped in confusion. I had no idea of where I was going, much less which way to turn. And the following morning, as Bête sat in patient wonderment, I threw her dog food to the birds.

I blamed the Prozac.

MARCH 22 TO APRIL 6

Henkelinda's next call came six days later, on March 27, from a refugee camp in Ljubljana. The line was bad and her English was even worse, if that was possible.

"What is happening?" I asked, but her only reply was, "say to Esad to call us."

Her voice, usually so full of life, was flat. She answered none of my questions.

"I want to come to America." she said. Of course, that's what I wanted too, but it was not possible and she knew it as well as I. There was a troubling note of whimper in her voice.

"Are you afraid?" I asked.

"Yes," she whispered.

This coming from the girl who had been through so much, whose smile was so broad, laugh so gurgling, and eyes so full of light. I was also afraid.

I was frantic to know what was happening. I used the number Esad had given me to pass her message on. A person named Joseph answered and promised to have Esad make the call but I heard nothing more from either of them. When I tried the number in Ljubljana that she was at, the phone slammed down after I said my first *hello.* Three more weeks dragged by.

If the family was in trouble – and they surely were – it was my fault. I'd interfered with their lives and tried my hand at playing God. I'd gone against the advice and counsel of people who worked with refugees and their problems. I'd tried and failed to buy a solution to the problems of these strangers who came from another world. I was feeling sick for them and sorry for myself.

Henkelinda didn't call again until April 16, and the little I could understand was all bad. Now they were in Koper, Slovenia, which nestled on my map against the Italian border near Trieste. They were out of money, had lost all their things and been totally deserted by the men who had promised them Western Europe in five days. She said something about a hospital – either Henkelinda or her mother had been in a hospital. She gave me their number and, as usual, the line went dead. Their luck had run out even as the luck of their fellow countrymen was improving.

AT 2:00 PM EST on March 24, the first NATO missiles had actually landed in Kosovo. Richard Holbrooke had left Belgrade the day before, his "final warning" (at least his most recent final warning) to Milosevic having had no effect. General Wesley Clark, NATO Supreme Commander, was in charge of the campaign. The Contact Group fell apart, with the U.S., France, Germany and the UK falling into step with NATO as a trio of Russian ministers rushed to Belgrade on March 30 for more "talks."

The three-phase NATO bombing campaign was aimed first at enemy air defense targets, next at the facilities and materials supplying the Kosovo hostilities and, finally, at central Belgrade. While the aim was to scare Milosevic into calling off his paramilitary goons, there was little impact on the ground activities themselves, where, by the first of April, 40,000 refugees could be seen on the road from Pristina to Macedonia and more than half a million civilians had been routed from their homes. On April 6, Milosevic announced his operations were completed and called for a cease fire but French President Chirac called a cease fire indefensible without a political agreement and security package, and NATO rejected the offer.

Although the first ten days had produced more than a hundred bombing hits, the overall war was not going well. There was the fear that Russia, who had dispatched warships from the Black Sea and pulled its SFOR troops in Bosnia out from under U.S. command, would actively join Serb forces. NATO troops stationed in Sarajevo – where there had been at least one Serbian attempt at an air strike – were considered in danger, and it occurred to me that American visitors to that city must be racing for the airport. Dick had not been so far wrong, after all.

The Russians weren't the only politicians looking for a way out. Talk of a bombing 'pause' began in Washington and elsewhere on Day Two, targets were withheld from the air forces until they'd gotten approvals from both the White House and NATO members, one allied plane had gone down, three soldiers in Macedonia were kidnaped, and several human errors had resulted in civilian casualties.

The NATO war appeared to be as off the mark as had been the earlier attempts to broker peace. The problem was on the ground in Kosovo, where heavily armed men were attacking, murdering and dispossessing civilians of their lives and property. The objective was to stop those men. But as a first step we sent in observers to document their misdeeds, then circled aircraft overhead to confirm the documentation and positioned armies at the border to pull them out. Next we convened masses of people and generated pages of documents in a far-away country, while more weaponry and manpower was brought in to continue the dirty work. And finally, here we were in an air campaign aimed at knocking out their air defenses which, until we launched our aircraft, hadn't contributed to the Kosovo problem at all. And as these vast resources of the western world bore down on Serbia, the people of Kosovo were still being swept away, out of their homes, toward their borders, out of their country where, as a ten million person diaspora, they would be even a greater problem for the western world. The military planners were not ignorant of the situation and, in the face of a universal political refusal to put troops on the ground, had called for Apache helicopters to provide the next best thing – troops just barely above the ground.

I had a very private personal dilemma. I wanted the bombing to succeed in driving the Serbian army out of Kosovo but if that happened, if the war was over, if the threat to the Albanians was eliminated, then the Bosnian camp would close and the refugees there would be back in their homes by summer. It would be good for those people, for Esad and his brother, for everyone except my friends. While my head and heart applauded the NATO campaign, my gut lagged behind in self-interested shame, as guts tend to do.

I still asked "Where are you, Henkelinda?" each morning, but my precious dog no longer lifted her black shaggy head to my voice. The vet – to be precise the vet's assistant, the boss being on vacation – had told me Bête was dying from kidney disease although I did not know how fast. She dragged herself around, collapsing at my feet when I sat at the computer, where I was doing very little writing and lots of game playing. It was breaking my heart. This was the first dog of my adult life and I treasured her more than I had dreamed possible when I had first brought her home as a puppy.

Any productivity in my life had come to a halt. As I brought the manuscript up on my screen, each morning, my mind began to gyrate with thoughts of Henkelinda and it was only the repetitive diversion of Tetris and Free Cell that could numb me into an artificial calm that helped the hours pass. I was marking time until something happened, and I didn't expect that something to be good.

I tried to pull myself back to work by attending a writer's seminar, submitting a short piece describing my first encounter with Henkelinda at the Hadžići camp. The class greeted it with polite interest, but a guy named Jim – a tough judgmental ex-priest – struck a blow.

"This is about a phony bleeding heart lady who fakes involvement with these people."

It was the best and worst thing I got out of the seminar. He had pricked the boil of my shame and all the puss came oozing out. It was a problem of character, not writing ability. I hadn't come to grips with what I'd done until this man, whom I hated for doing it, said it out loud. I'd been too taken with the idea of what I was doing to get it done. I had to make things happen. The hell with writing, the hell with Prozac, I needed to tackle this thing head on.

APRIL 7 TO MAY 19

My conversations with Henkelinda were useless. I had to get others involved. I called Joseph and asked him for his help in finding out what the UNHCR in Sarajevo could do for the family. He agreed to call both Henkelinda and the UN folks but when I asked about Esad, Joseph was angry.

"Kosovars are charming," the missionary said, "but very manipulative." I assumed that Esad had manipulated me – who wouldn't have in his situation – but had he manipulated Joseph too?"

"His brother cries all the time and Esad doesn't seem to care," continued Joseph. Clearly, Esad was out of grace, and I let a week go by before I called again.

Joseph's news, on April 16, was gloomy. Henkelinda and her family were living in an old peoples' home in Slovenia, with several other Albanian families, hoping to get across the border into Italy. They hadn't made it and this dead end was no better than the Coca Cola camp – no, without the help of the United Nations, it was worse. Because Henkelinda's family had voluntarily left the camp, they were on their own and the UNHCR people in Sarajevo could be of no help. Joseph promised to talk to them again and before he hung up he passed along news of Esad – gangs in the camp had heard about his money and were after him. I had caused trouble for Esad too.

I had a lot to straighten out. I started by spending days on the phone looking for legal ways to extradite the family from Slovenia. I called my Congressman whose staffer knew from personal experience about refugee programs and was very helpful, forwarding me to others at the state department, refugee assistance agencies, the Office of Refugee Resettlement, and the Kosovo project at the Kent College of Law. They only reinforced what Ann Sides had told me six months before in Sarajevo – that Kosovars would be struck by lightning before being accepted in the U.S. as refugees. Every path dead ended. The old ideas were rehashed: if Henkelinda could get to a UNHCR processing point, she could file a request for resettlement in a European country. Even if such a request was granted, which was very unlikely, there was no UN facility in Slovenia. The closest was in Zagreb, from whence the police had chased them out.

I talked to NONA ("Grandmother"), who was helping refugees in Zagreb; to CESTRA, the PTSD Alliance and Crisis Intervention; to all the NGOs with psycho-social programs working with refugees. Someone with CESTRA suggested trying the political asylum route – if they could get to an American consulate and ask for political asylum, I was told, it might be granted, but the likelihood was slim, more like a crap shoot. Then I heard about a girl who got into the United States illegally and asked for asylum. She was still sitting in the federal prison in Chicago, waiting for her case to be reviewed. I dropped the idea. I sent a letter to the State Department and was told to wait a month for a response. I tried a hotline number without success, and was referred to Interchurch Refugees and Interchurch Ministries, who did not return my call.

Then, in early May, I heard that the U.S. was starting to allow Kosovar refugees into the country. A lightning strike! I called Sandra Stratton, at Refugee Services of South Bend, the closest official distribution agency for refugees. I asked if I could officially sponsor Henkelinda's family and I learned our policy was restricted to Kosovars living in the Macedonian tent camps set up by UNHCR. The program was designed to ease the pressure on the Macedonians as well as help the Kosovars. It became clear that without a legal alternative, the solution was to make the illegal one work.

A lawyer friend suggested that I go to Italy and smuggle them across the border myself.

"Will you go with me?"

"No, but when you land in jail, I'll come and get you out."

"Very funny!"

But I wondered, could I do a thing like that? I have driven so easily across European borders, flashing my dark blue passport at border guards who waved me through. But with eight Kosovar refugees in the car? I began to think about it seriously. Broke and deserted, they were helpless. The only way I could get them money was to hand deliver it. This was the final test for me, one that I'd probably fail. No more than I had been willing to exchange my comfortable hotel room for their freezing tent, that night in Sarajevo, would I be willing to risk jail for them. If that was true I really was a fraud. That ex-priest was righter than he knew.

But I didn't have to take that test, as things moved forward without help from me. Joseph called to say that Esad had asked Christ to be his savior, changed his name to Eddie, and sent his share of the money to Henkelinda in Koper. Religion was good for something, after all. Eddie/Esad was back in Joseph's good graces and Joseph in mine. In the second week of May Joseph called again to say that Henkelinda had gotten the money but was in the hospital with kidney stones.

"Kosovars often get kidney stones," he said in his latest all-knowing pronouncement.

I was too grateful to him to object. I hadn't talked to Henkelinda for almost a month, while Joseph with his Albanian language skills had done it all. I dropped the idea of going to Italy – at least for now – and waited.

The war had deteriorated into a series of anecdotal news stories, mainly associated with collateral damage: a bus full of civilians was hit on a bridge north of Pristina, as were 80 Kosovars holed up in what appeared to be a military compound in the town of Kornica, and as NATO intensified its attack on Belgrade strategic targets, it destroyed the infamous Target #493, the new Chinese embassy, killing three and wounding 20. The building had been identified by a CIA agent who hadn't been in Belgrade for several years, and although Clark protested in vain that it was an accident and argued that the record of less than ten serious mistakes in over a thousand air strikes was good, the western community was up in arms. Nerves in the Belgrade diplomatic community were so frayed that the Ukrainians sent NATO the address of their new Embassy. Public resistance to the war was growing and the populations of many western nations joined China in street protests. Even Milica fired off an angry e-mail to me from Sarajevo: "how can they say these killings are mistakes!" she wrote, referring to Serbian deaths from NATO bombings. I, in turn, wondered how she, a beneficiary of former NATO air attacks, could say otherwise.

Peace plans abounded – initiatives put forth by Germany and Russia, a plan from the G8 countries, cease fires proposed by the Italians and by the Greeks. Yugoslavia appealed to the world court to stop the air strike genocide. When Chicago's Jesse Jackson emerged from Belgrade with the released three kidnaped airmen, there was worry about what he might have promised in return.

The fact was, the air war was running out of steam. While the number of aircraft increased – almost 600 were involved in late April – the number of approved targets diminished. Serbs on the ground in Kosovo had gotten smarter at keeping their assets away from NATO aircraft, and earlier estimates of the number of civilians hiding out in the mountains had doubled and were estimated at 800,000 by late April. The Apache helicopters being readied in Albania had suffered two losses in training missions and Washington was stonewalling their further use. The issue whose debate behind closed doors was hot and heavy occasionally leaked out into the pages of the press – when would ground forces be sent in? Blair and Clinton were rumored to have had a "stormy discussion" on the subject and Clark was battling both his superiors and subordinates, arguing that if there was to be a victory before the next winter, ground troops must invade by July and a mid-summer invasion required planning to begin immediately. Clark was not invited to a NATO 50th anniversary summit on April 23 and a ground invasion was not even discussed. Four days later, when the General reviewed the options, including ground troops, before the European press, he got a call from his Pentagon boss telling him: *get your fucking face off the TV.* Wesley Clark wasn't doing any better than was I.

My private life had totally fallen apart. I spent all my waking hours for two solid days playing Tetris; ate an entire carton of ice cream and jar of chocolate sauce in one sitting, and started guzzling martinis as I watched the nightly TV shots of thousands of Kosovars streaming southward toward the border in Milosevic's final ethnic cleansing sweep. Bête wasn't there to hear me question Henkelinda's picture for several mornings. She was in the animal hospital for treatment and then sent home to die. I'd stopped writing all together and the only constructive thing I did the last week in April was cut bushes in my woods and come home loaded with ticks. I blamed everything on the Prozac and began to cut back on the dosage. Thanks to my meddling, eight Kosovars were beyond the help of the international UNHCR and miles from the one spot from which the U.S. was now accepting Kosovar refugees – the camps in Macedonia. I spoke of my failure to a friend.

"Why don't you sponsor one of those Macedonian families?" Jeanette asked, perhaps a bit cynically, "if the Kosovars are so important to you?"

It was Henkelinda, not just any Kosovar, that was important to me, but I wasn't willing to admit it. I began to work with Sandra Stratton in South Bend to bring over such a family, organizing a local sponsoring group. It gave me a place to channel my miseries.

MAY 19 TO JUNE 20

And then it was over. On May 19, Henkelinda called from Germany, where it was two o'clock in the morning.

"How did you do it?" I asked, but she only laughed and in her throaty English said, over and over, "we are in Germany."

A miracle!

I got the next call on May 24, from a refugee camp in the northern German town of Dortmund. They had applied for asylum and had no idea what would happen next. But they were safe, had food and shelter. The worst was behind them. Over the next week my phone rang three times at 4 AM, but the line was always dead, and when she finally reached me, from a new refugee camp in Oldenburg, the situation overwhelmed her pigeon-English. They would be moved again, not knowing when or where. The only way to find out what was happening was to talk face to face. I made a plan to be there on July 3.

No less a miracle was occurring in the Balkans. Right after Henkelinda arrived in Stuttgart, NATO began bombing the Yugoslav electricity grid, affecting every aspect of Serbian life. By the end of May, Russia's Chernomyrdin and the Finnish Marti Ahtisaari were in Belgrade proposing the G-8's principles for peace: a cease-fire, withdrawal of Serbian forces from Kosovo, return of the refugees, a NATO-led presence in Kosovo and Serbian participation in a political settlement.

On June 3, Milosevic agreed to accept the principles but during the next week, to no one's surprise, it was politically touch and go. As Belgrade balked, NATO intensified the bombing and international diplomacy was in full force, with Germany, Russia, and NATO all involved. On June 9, protracted meetings in Macedonia produced a military technical agreement and the following day, Serbian troops began their withdrawal from northern Kosovo. After 77 days of the air campaign NATO ordered the air strikes suspended at 10:00 AM EST, June 10, and the UN passed Resolution 1244 endorsing the major principles of the agreement. On June 20 NATO officially ended the bombings and thus ended the war. Shortly thereafter, Europe witnessed the largest spontaneous return of refugees since WW II. They did not include Henkelinda and her family.

But at least they were safe in Western Europe, so I confronted the other problems in my life. I threw the remaining Prozac tablets into the trash, deleted all the games from my computer and set myself a new writing schedule. Then I called the vet.

"Is there something I can give my dog to ease the pain?" I asked. It was the first time I had spoken to him directly about my pet. There was a pause on the other end of the line as he reviewed the file.

"Get her in here right away," he said, "I want to do some tests."

Bete Noire

Twenty four hours later, Bête was back from the dead. The vet had diagnosed what his assistant had not: Addison's Disease. Fatal if not treated, it was a glandular thing – the remedy was easy, once the problem was correctly identified. My dog and I were on the road back to the good life, having taken a dreadful detour. Henkelinda and her family were safe and although the war had ended with good results, living conditions in Germany were probably better than in her homeland. I'd find that out in early July, when I visited.

I was mildly jubilant and inordinately relieved. Those five months had taken a toll. I'd worked hard for the results but it could just as easily have turned out differently. It had been too big a risk, too bold a step for me to handle. Maybe I should try to get my old job back. I was running scared.

But I had a new problem. I'd gotten a call from Sandra that among the last Albanian Kosovar families coming to the U.S. from Macedonian camps was one on its way to us. Their name was Mehmeti and they would be here in six days.

CHAPTER 7

THE GROUP

What happened next involved very little thinking. The impulse born in the Coca Cola camp the previous fall propelled me from 17-year old Henkelinda to 42-year-old Hatixhe without a hitch. In the spring of 1999, as the nightly newscasts increased their coverage of endless miles of Kosovar refugees wheeling their possessions toward the Macedonia border in carts, trucks and tractor drawn wagons, the State Department had finally announced that up to 25,000 refugees would be accepted into the United States from the UNHCR tent camps.

The ruling did not apply to Kosovar refugees stuck in the no man's land of Slovenia, no more than to those who had landed in Germany. It applied only to people living in the Macedonian camps.

When my fried, Jeanette, had challenged me to sponsor one of those refugee families "if I cared so much about Kosovars," I'd taken the challenge, giving little thought to what it might entail.

Sandra Stratton, at the South Bend Refugee Agency, had told me applications for refugee sponsorship were being accepted from qualified groups.

"What qualifies a group?" I asked. Sandra usually dealt with church groups but answered that any dozen people could constitute such a group – she was thinking out loud – as long as their resources were enough to support a refugee family's needs.

There was such overwhelming sympathy for Kosovars among my television-watching friends that twelve telephone calls brought fourteen people to my house, one evening, to form a "group". One of those first attendees organized her church to sponsor a second refugee family and another simply dropped out, so by the time Sandra came to look us over, we were down to twelve. We were Christians, Jews, one Muslim and several atheists; married, single, widowed and divorced; rich and poor; more women than men. We were long on energy. One of us – saints be praised – spoke some Serbian. I was the official sponsor and would provide the house – the old farmhouse 50 yards from my front door where my visiting children and grandchildren stayed. Free food, clothes, household furnishings, and even two cars came pouring in. No significant cash outlays should be required.

"The family will require lots of support services," Sandra warned as she passed around a thirty-item preliminary check list, "and you'll need to shepherd them through a maze of government red tape."

"No problem," we said, more with our hearts than heads.

"And then," she added, "there are the unpredictable, the special needs of any given family," but how could one have a conversation about them? We were, in the words of Linda, a group member, "all geeked up" and nothing could deter us.

Our sponsorship application was processed and approved and we set about our self-assigned tasks. On June 7th Sandra called to say that an extended family of six had been referred to us, including 9-month old twins. We added diapers and car seats to our list of needs. Two days later we learned that through a bureaucratic snafu, that family had been sent to Tennessee. The enthusiasm of the group member whose car trunk was loaded with diapers temporarily waned.

When the cease fire was announced, June 10th, our happiness at the war's end was tempered by disappointment that there might be no family for us. Secretly, I was relieved. I knew by then some of the ways in which my life might be turned upside down.

Among the million things I like about my life, the best is solitude. I sleep while others are still working in their gardens and read history at sunrise, before they wake. I watch the constellations wheel across the sky on clear nights from my bed and bathe in the primal freshness of each morning's sunrise walk to the barn.

"Good morning," I call to the assembled hungry critters, and they always answer back, in tongues.

Some prefer such pleasures in the company of others, but I do not. People, although I like them well enough in other settings, distract me from the pleasures of my private life. After the emotional roller coaster of the spring I wanted extra solitude in which to lick my wounds. I could throw this over only because I had wanted something more, something that had been set in motion in the Coca Cola camp. But our reprieve from the first family had given me time to think.

———

Already the farm house was full of activity that had no connection with me. Bête was hoarse from protective barking, the heads of the horse and goats hung over the fence in unending curiosity and the chickens squawked and fluttered before the cars that came and went. A living breathing family in that house might bring bedlam to my life. But *the moving finger writes* – a family was on its way.

The day after the cease fire Sandra received new paperwork, enlivened with black and white photos of three school age boys and their parents, our Kosovars. They looked solemn and very sad. I hoped they would be nice.

We were given 48 hours' notice of their arrival and on June 25th nine of us went to the South Bend airport in two vans, jammed in among a mass of red helium balloons and a large banner that read MIRESE ARDMET FAMILIA MEHMETI NE AMERIKA which meant, we hoped, "Welcome to the Mehmeti family to America."

The Group greets the family in South Bend

Jammed in among us were two Albanian-speaking teenagers whose parents had emigrated from Montenegro years before. In "The Group," (now our official name) was our Serbian speaker, Eva, whose mother had lived in Yugoslavia when it was one country with one language. The language of the others was tears and smiles.

The flight was delayed and we had too much time to pace and chatter and worry and wonder, before our family straggled through the arrival gate. Our well-fed, happy hodgepodge group waved and grinned over the top of the banner, flashing cameras in their startled eyes. First came the boys, skinny and uneasy, the older two flickering self-conscious smiles, the youngest half hidden behind his mother and glaring at the floor. Oh Lord, I thought, thinking of Henkelinda's youngest brother, another little Kosovar boy who hates me!

The Mehmeti's arrival in South Bend

The father stepped forward to shake our hands, a handsome bearded man in work pants and a thin collared shirt sharply creased from the cardboard from which it must have been unfolded minutes before. But my eyes were on the woman, whose solemn face was drawn long and taut, her large eyes fixed unhappily on us, as someone thrust a bouquet of flowers into her unenthusiastic arms. She looked from face to face, not so much scared as deeply exhausted, barely able to lift the corners of her lips into the smallest smile. This was a serious and thoughtful woman, I thought, who is going to be – I was sure of it – my friend! My emotions raced through relief and on to joy.

When we looked back later at that airport meeting, we saw ourselves through their eyes across a chasm which they faced at the end of a long and difficult journey. It had begun 36 hours earlier in a plane chock full of excitement and relief at leaving the camps. Their first flight had been from Skopje, Macedonia to Athens, where they waited many hours for the plane to JFK airport in New York, a commercial flight and away from many of their compatriots who had shared the chartered first one. In New York, still buttressed by fellow refugees, they had processed reams of paperwork with the help of a translator and were sent, this time alone, to another airport by bus. They had 40 DM which they exchanged for $18. The youngest boy was hungry and bought a hamburger and coke, receiving $5 in change. *How shall we survive in this wealthy country?* His father wondered.

The next leg was to Pittsburgh where they were met by someone who gave them more food. The last leg was a puddle jumper to South Bend. They had never heard of South Bend, Indiana, nor seen it on a map. When their plane was delayed they gave up any hope of being met.

When she told me this, much later, this woman whose name, Hatixhe, was commonly shortened to Hata, I was shocked.

"You thought you would be stranded in a place you'd never heard of? Weren't you terrified?" I asked.

"Not me," she said. "We were together, we had eaten and, for the first time in a decade, we felt safe." These Kosovar women, I thought, are made of sturdy stuff.

During the summer of 1999, in Indiana, the heat did not let up. The two ancient air conditioners that ground away in the windows of the little farm house were useless, and the Mehmeti family, The Group and countless volunteers who materialized out of the community to bring gifts and teach English spent much of the days at the picnic table under the trees. The days were long and highly scheduled, with comings and goings of the family members to government agencies, doctors and clinics, schools and stores. I set up a schedule of events and participants and faxed it out to members of The Group. It was so complicated and changed so frequently, it was the only time I've ever added the "hour" to the date/time insert on my computer. It was a busy summer. Hata worked ceaselessly, cooking, baking bread, cleaning the little house and washing the clothes that she hung out on the long chain link fence along the road. The boys worked with vacationing elementary school teachers who gave hours of help each week, went to a soccer camp enrolled in by members of The Group, kicked balls about the yard and, in evening's coolness, bounced a ball on the basketball court between our houses. The youngest, Luan, rode a tiny donated bicycle up and down the driveway from my house to the road. Up and down, up and down, up and down. When he was outdoors, which was most of every day, I kept Bête inside. The boy had been threatened by Serbian soldiers with an attack dog – "if you move, it will kill you," they had said, and he was terrified of dogs. And what did Xhela do? He paced the floor. The late night light in the kitchen betrayed his sleeplessness; he chain smoked, and he worried so incessantly about his family, friends and country that he couldn't concentrate on the simplest English lesson. While his sons and even his wife picked up, with time and effort through the summer, enough of the language to begin to survive on their own, he was learning very little.

Xhela's tragedy was the greatest. He had been an important man in Kosovo, had had a good job with lots of authority – was manager of 500 men and driven to work each day by a chauffeur, – here he had no work, that which gives a man his greatest value. He had an important role there, not here. Out of frustration and rage he tackled the shrubbery around my house with saw and scythe . . . defoliating all the low branches of the pines along the road that

I had carefully preserved for privacy. It didn't matter. His need was big. Mine was not. He was on the phone overseas continually, searching out the members of his family who had scattered as he had, sending one brother as far away as Australia. They all eventually went home – but he did not.

It is the man that suffers in a dislocation – he is too culture- and language-dependent, while the woman brings her work and worth with her, to sustain the family; to keep the children and her husband alive, well fed, warm, clean and cared for. The boys went to her for comfort as well as strength. She was the rock, the strong and sturdy one. Sitting with her, one day, a report of atrocities at home brought tears streaming down her cheeks but when I reached out to touch she pushed my hand away. Her grief was hers alone and that was how she would and could handle it.

Hating every minute of it, she learned the ways of the Laundromat, the grocery store, the local Walmart. She worked through the English lessons, sorted through the well-stocked shelves, threw out all the canned goods containing pork and others with which they were unfamiliar – who would have thought baked beans and peanut butter would have been rejected? Sheets from one boy's bed appeared on the clothesline, which we had rigged from fence to house, each morning faithfully. There were terrors of war contained inside the house of which we'd never know.

Xhela, on the other hand, roaming the grounds, jumping up from the table during lessons, growling at the boys in Albanian, took the driver's license test three times before he passed. Although the language was not a problem in the examination (he was allowed a translator) it had been a problem in the learning, as he insisted that he understood the *left hand turn only* sign. He had no idea what it meant, didn't understand our explanation and denied that he didn't understand. To the question "Do you understand?" Xhela's answer was always "yes". His pride would not allow it to be otherwise.

There was eventually a front page story in the local paper, which generated lots of offers of help. People stopped by with clothes, with food, with comments . . .always well-intentioned but sometimes offensive. At the sign of a strange car parked by their house I'd hurry out, to ward off possible disasters. Some people brought junk – ugly, used things, expecting gratitude. Others insulted in a different way – I collected the Christian bibles as rapidly as they arrived. They fared no better at the hands of fellow Muslims. You'll come to mosque with us, yes? No, we don't go to Mosque, they answered. Not acceptable.

Many in the town had a naive notion of Kosovo- a third world country, they'd call it. No, it's European, I'd say, do you think Europe is third world?

How nice for them to be out there on the farm with all those animals, they'd say.

Actually, they don't like the animals at all – they lived in a city apartment and aren't comfortable with horse manure so close. As for the dog . . . less said the better.

Those people are such good workers, one commented watching Hata help me move bales of hay – she'd come outside when she saw the truck arrive – she looked for ways to help me, as I did her, and both of us could do the work of men.

No, *this* person is a good worker. *Those* people are just like us – some work hard, some don't.

The group had its own problems with them – we had a hard time dealing with their sense of entitlement. We wanted gratitude instead. We'd done so much, provided so much and what we didn't, the government did. They had food stamps, welfare, medicaid, and, thanks to us, they'd be able to salt much of it away. We got a bit sniffy with the boys when they wanted gym shoes like the other boys – or with Hata and Xhela when they stuffed the clothes we got them, often bought new, into garbage bags for the Salvation Army. We got two free cars, one of which they thought too old and decrepit.

We looked for jobs for them. We looked and looked and looked. We went with them on interviews, wrote letters, made phone calls, and the fact that nothing materialized, or at least nothing good enough, drove us to the brink. "Knowing someone" was the way to get a job in Kosovo, we surmised, and they couldn't understand a system where influence and clout didn't produce. We tried to pull the strings we had, but they mostly broke in our fingers. As Xhela saw it, either we had no influence or we weren't willing to use it for them.

"If you came to my country, MY group would get you a good job," Xhela told me once in frustration.

Less than a mile away was a blueberry farm run by a new owner who was struggling to find enough pickers for the fruit. It was a perfect fit for the Albanian speaking family and I would often see the farm owners' car in the driveway before 7 AM, taking various members of the family off to work. Although the Mehmetis neither knew nor liked blueberries, it worked out well. "We never could have made it through that first summer without them," reminisces Diane, the owner's wife, and it gave the refugees a welcome activity and a little cash.

By fall, they'd settled into a routine. Xhela had a job- machinist at minimum wage – and a driver's license. The job had come, in fact, as a favor from someone our group member, Richard, knew. Hata began by cleaning houses, a circumstance that embarrassed them all. She'd had an important supervisory job in Kosovo. The three boys went to three different schools – picked up by yellow buses at the end of the driveway. We'd laid the groundwork. Principals, teachers and a scattering of new friends were waiting for them, and a very special third grade teacher assigned an aide to work with Luan exclusively – until his natural abilities propelled him to the head of the class and he didn't need her any more. In junior high school the middle boy had made the honor role by mid-year. No problems there.

Things were settling down in Kosovo, the United Nations Force (KFOR) was patrolling the streets, NGO's were pouring money and workers into rebuilding the infra-structure, and a local government was beginning to materialize. The United States offered – encouraged – refugees to return home. The Mehmetis had the right to stay here, get green cards and eventually to become U.S. citizens. It was a rare opportunity, particularly for the boys, but Xhela was thinking about going home. I was distressed, thinking of how desperately Henkelinda and her family wanted the chance to immigrant.

Xhela was suffering too much from the severance of his roots to feel comfortable here at first. Not Hata. She wanted to stay. She wanted it for the boys: the better life, the better education, the better health care, but it was more than that. She had lost everything by leaving there EXCEPT her family – but somehow she'd be able to make it over here, make a life for herself. I knew a lot about Hata now because I had become her friend.

Hata had made real friends with several of the women of The Group, warm personal relationships with give and take. In me she saw a mother substitute. It was only partly an age thing. Hata was almost ten years older than my children; on the other hand, her mother was younger than me. I had played the role of sponsor, of teacher and mentor and finally of friend. We went to the schools, agencies and clinics together, as she struggled with the health, emotional and academic issues that come with motherhood. I walked her through the cultural differences and soon enough she was on her own firm ground, dealing with those motherhood issues. Should she trust this doctor's diagnosis or look for a second opinion? could she count on that teacher's understanding her son? should she take this counselor's advice? These were cross-cultural issues that made up the stuff, around the world, of raising children, and she and I tended to see most things as one. Walking out of a dentist's office, one day, after a particularly officious pronouncement by the doctor, we turned to each other and simultaneously scrunched our faces in disgust. We had the kind of compatibility that made for friendship of a deep and trusting kind. She'd usually ask my opinion and I'd always tell her what I thought but it was understood that final decisions were hers, that I had no business on that side of the line. We were friends. And as her friend, I knew about her relationship with her husband, how strenuously she avoided conflict, how important it was that he maintain authority in their home.

Everything they had been, up until now, was in that little piece of Eastern Europe wedged between Montenegro, Macedonia, Albania and Serbia and slanted toward the Adriatic Sea. Life had been hell there for the last ten years but it was where the parents had their roots, it was their everlasting home. Both had escaped the more conventional lives of their brothers and sisters to attend the university in Pristina, Kosovo's capital. For Xhela, to break free from family tradition to become an engineer was ground breaking enough; for Hata, the only female engineer in her graduating class, it was remarkable. And when they married – outside of family oversight, into families from other regions, by falling in love, they broke the mold. They did not return to Xhela's family home, where Hata would have joined the other daughters in law in baking bread and making pita, in living and raising children in the large, safe, comfortable extended family environment. Instead, they moved into an apartment in Skenderai, an apartment of their own. They both had jobs – good jobs – and one by one the children came. Before it all began to fall apart, they'd had a good and happy life, and even after the suffering inflicted on Albanians by Milosevic, that piece of land was home, with all the precious sanctity that word imputes. They, as everyone in the world since time began, saw life as being rich and whole and happy only on one particular piece of earth – the one called home.

The Mehmetis had changed my life. At least they commandeered it. The useful work I did for the first summer, and much of the fall, winter and spring that followed, was with and for them. The externals were only part of it – from where I sat at my computer, I watched Luan wobble up and down the drive on the bike; the older boys bounce the basketball on the court. Knocks came at my door into the evening – only the morning hours, before eight, that is, were ones I could truly call my own. People came with questions, clothes and food, not all of which were helpful. Our Group disintegrated until there remained a core whose solidarity made up for the breakdown of the rest. Our problem was the difficulty of making decisions that affected someone else's life. And here we had ambivalence. Hata and the boys were eager for our advice and counsel – often too much so. Xhela, on the other hand, had ideas that could not be swayed by what, in our minds, was expertise in the ways of his new world. He forbade his oldest son, a high school junior, to date. He climbed into an unregistered car one day, although still without a license to drive, and took off down the road.

There were life-affecting issues . . . where should the boys go to school, their curriculum; should the family return to Kosovo or stay? should we push Xhela to hold out for a better job or should he take just anything, working on his English until he qualified for higher pay. Life's decisions are hard enough to make for oneself and one's dependents. To make them for another family – not only impossible, but impossible for a group to make. Each of us had a different notion of the control that we should exert, when we should insist, when we should step back. The four of us that stayed intact were closest in our approach to that issue, and we tended toward the laissez faire, tempered with the love that we felt. We always think – not always correctly – that if we love enough, our interference in other peoples' lives is for the best.

All the information about them came later in dribs and drabs that expanded as their English vocabularies did. Our first attempts to understand their history were failures. I would go to their house, evenings that first summer, with my pad and pen, to record what the father, reading from cramped scribbled notes, would communicate through a translator, with the family sitting around the table. But those sessions, with their resurrection of past traumas, would end in Albanian discussions and debates that left me in both the cold and dark. Confused chronologies, politics, rage and terror created a maelstrom into which all information was sucked. It was only much later, when Hata and I could sit quietly together, that I was able to interpret the content of those discussions and piece together the recent history of this family. It had much in common with the story Henkelinda had told.

CHAPTER 8

HATA'S STORY

They had come to the South Bend airport after three months in a Macedonian tent city, where it had rained all through that colder-than-normal spring, but their suffering went back a decade to 1989, when Milosevic took away the semi-autonomous privileges that Kosovar Albanians had enjoyed since 1968. Among the family's earliest losses was Hata's job. In the munitions factory where she'd been a supervisor, only Serbians were now allowed to work. It was much more than a munitions factory, she knew. As early as 1991, when she had still been working, it harbored an underground munitions depot and a shelter for soldiers, and was visited by Arkan (Željko Ražnatović), the paramilitary thug who was later indicted by the ICTY for war crimes in Bosnia, where he operated as the leader of a murderous group known as Arkan's tigers.

The Drenica area, where Skenderaj (called Srbica, the Serbian name, back then) was located, was a center of guerilla resistance and police oppression. The two went hand in hand. As the Albanians' rights were systematically removed, the resistance movement developed that was known as the UCK to them, the KLA to us. Terrorists to the Serbs, freedom fighters to the Albanians, they increased their activities as the police cracked down, forcing even more men to go underground. In 1996 two Skenderaj men had been abducted and tortured before being jailed and by 1997 there were rumblings of big trouble ahead. In September the police secretly picked up a local man, Gani Thaqi, on the streets of the town and later came back to rough up his old father and bulldoze his yard in a search for guns. Skerderaj quickly became a hotbed of violence, perpetrated by both sides.

Toward the end of 1997, Arkan began to show up around town, staying in the hotel associated with the munitions factory and driving around in an armored car. Someone heard him say that since the Yugoslavian army couldn't get rid of the Albanians, he'd taken on the job himself. Maybe it was only rumor, Hata admitted, or maybe not.

On January 28, 1998, at 4:30 A.M. the first shivers of terror affected the Mehmeti family. They were eating breakfast in their apartment in the five story building perched on the hill that rises westward from the main street – it was Ramadan and they were up to eat before sunrise – and his mother was visiting. There was gunfire outside, frightening the old woman, but they told her it was nothing and sent her back to bed. Peering into the hall, Xhela saw police running up the stairs past the apartment. He quickly shut the door and they sat there terrified. They had no idea what was happening then or even later – the air in town was so thick with fear that no one dared cut through it with questions.

The next events, as described by Xhela and Hata, were vaguely familiar to me, the very same massacres I'd heard about on CNN so many months before. They talked about the Ahmetis, who lost eleven men, according to Xhela, from 12 to 60 years old. Xhela had been at the University of Pristina with Ilmi Ahmeti and, the latter being the city consultant to the region, Xhela saw him often and knew him well. When the news of the massacre reached Skenderaj, Xhela and other men from town went in a bus to Likosane. Walking across a field toward the Ahmeti house he saw human teeth and brains lying on the ground. Several corpses were still lying where they fell – the bodies of a man and pregnant woman rested inside one house, by the stove.

"They picked the most successful homes, the ones with the most men," Xhela told me. He visited the matriarch of the Ahmeti family, an old woman whose four sons, sons in law and grandson had been taken away.

"Please leave me my grandson," she had begged the police. He was 11 years old.

"We will bring him back," they had answered and they did, but it was in a body bag.

Xhela and the other men buried the dead.

In the first week in March, the war came to Skenderaj and the nearby towns of Prekaze and Llausha and it was also a story I had heard before.

"They came to get Adem Jashair." said Xhela. "They had tried three times before but he was never home. This time they found him at home, with his three brothers and their families." Xhela also knew Adem well, had been with him for three years in the Middle Technical School.

The Jashari were well equipped with guns and fought back during a siege of their homes that lasted five days, during which time the Mehmetis and their neighbors never left their own homes. Replacements were brought in for soldiers who were killed. When the Jashari family finally ran out of ammunition on March 9th, they all were killed – 20 of them: seven adults and 13 children, and numerous others who had tried to join the fight were also dead.

The Serbian commander called the village head man, Zuk Jashari (related but not closely to the victims, although his own son had been killed in the battle) to his office.

"If you want to bury them you can, or we will do it," he said.

"If you let us bury them with our traditions, in a religious ceremony, we will do it," was his answer, but the Commander refused. The soldiers took three trucks filled with the bodies, according to Zuk, and using the prisoners from the jail to do the work at night, they dug the graves in a row with a machine, in lower Prekaze. Several days later the people of the town opened the graves and reburied them, in a religious ceremony.

From then on the Mehmetis lived in fear. It was impossible to maintain a normal life. Fidan, their oldest boy, had been in school with three of the Jashari girls – two had died in the battle and the third, a 16-year-old, ran away to join the UCK. Hata and Xhela were afraid for him, both for his safety and for his mental health. They sent him and his brother Alban east to live with her mother, in a safer area of Kosovo, Gjilan. Little Luan stayed at home with his parents.

In early June the police came to a neighboring family of women and children, flourished their knives and said "we are going to cut your throats," although they left them unharmed. Such incidents created an atmosphere of unending dread for what might happen next.

On June 10, 1998 the paramilitary came and threw the families that remained in Skerderaj out of their apartments; the Mehmetis lived in the mountains for the following 128 days. (It was during this time that Luan became terrified of the men in uniform, who would sharpen their knives and threaten to cut throats.) They were constantly on the move. The women had flour with which to make bread, along with salt and noodles and water from springs along the way. Sometimes they slept in a house, but more often on or under (in case of rain) the trailers that moved with them. They were harassed by the Serbian military and Hata heard reports of killings. Parents of girls worried about rape and one woman covered her daughter's face with mud and put a scarf on her head to resemble an old woman.

"I was always thinking about Fidan and Alban," Hata said, "and how we could get to them."

One night when they had access to a TV they heard about the international monitors coming to Kosovo and, according to Hata, everyone believed the war would come to an end.

On October 8th they headed back home and four days later NATO passed the resolution authorizing air strikes; it was Solana's announcement of that action that Mary and I had heard from our hotel beds in Zagreb. The agreement reached the next day, just words to us who heard them on CNN the following night, had major significance for the Mehmetis. It was agreed that OSCE would put 2,000 "verifiers" on the ground and use air reconnaissance to further verify that the agreement was being adhered to. This Kosovo Verification Mission (KVM) was to be headed up by William Walker. Full compliance with the agreement was expected by Tuesday, October 27th, according to NATO commander Wesley Clark. The "agreement" spelled out the specifics of withdrawal of Serbian armed forces from Kosovo. On the night of October 27th Mary and I had sat in Sarajevo, watching a TV report that the Albanian people were coming out of the forest and going back into their homes. Those people had included three who were now part of my life – Hata, Xhela and Luan.

"Now we knew the war would stop," said Hata, "because the United States was involved and they would make the other countries help. We knew and loved Madeline Albright and Bill Clinton; also Richard Holbrook and Kofi Annan and Wesley Clark. But our favorite was William Walker!"

The Serbians knew about the American role as well. Hata remembers an angry paramilitary shouting at her, "You are calling on Americans to kill us!"

Hata told me that from October until March 1999, while the monitors were in the country, things were calm, although everyone knew that Serbia was amassing troops on the northern border of the province. There had been the last ditch effort in Rambouillet from the 6th to the 23rd of February and in Paris from the 15th to the 18th of March. On March 19 and 20th the monitors left, the Serbian military surged in and on March 20, at 9:45 A.M., the paramilitary took the people from their homes. Some were killed. From their apartment they saw eight men shot in the street.

It was on that day, March 20th, that the most frightening moment for the Mehmetis came, when Xhela, Hata and Luan were in the apartment. The police had entered the building and were systematically going from door to door, taking all the men. A young woman from a neighboring apartment asked Luan to visit them.

"It will be better if he is not there to see them take Xhela," she said to Hata. But Luan, as small children often do, knew what was happening.

"If they ask for money," he told his mother as he left, "give them every last penny."

Just before the police pounded at their door, Xhela stuffed himself into the large, stand-alone freezer. When Hata opened the door they searched the apartment looking for the "man of the house" in vain.

"He is at work," she said. They took the money that she had only half-hidden (which did not include "every last penny") and eventually they left. Soon after, Luan returned. All three of them had believed that Xhela would be killed.

In the meantime Holbrook was back in Belgrade, trying to convince Milosevic to stop the attacks on the Kosovars, in order to avoid NATO air strikes. Milosevic refused to comply and on March 23rd air strikes began. Between the 20th and 24th the Mehmetis had the impression that there were tanks (including Russian ones), bombing, and police everywhere.

"I will remember every minute of March 24th for the rest of my life," Hata says today. On that day she, Xhela and Luan, along with many of their neighbors, left Skenderaj for good. Xhela wanted to stay but Hata insisted that he join them. She found a bus that was headed for Mitrovica, to the north, and asked the Serbian bus driver if it would be safe for them to travel there. He said it would, and, in a sympathetic gesture, refused to take any money for their fares. In Mitrovica they were uncertain how to continue and ended up squeezing onto a bus headed for Pristina. It was full of Serbians and the terrified Mehmetis kept very quiet during the trip.

At a roadblock a military called out to the conductor, "Do you have anything?" and was answered "No, nothing."

The "anything" that they were talking about was Albanians, said Hata, "and I was so frightened I was shaking."

Pristina was filled with people and cars but they found a crowded bus headed for Gjilan. Again, the bus was full of Serbians and they survived more roadblocks.

Leaving the bus in the center of Gjilan, the town was full of soldiers in camouflage, with branches on their heads.

"Imagine, branches on their heads," said Hata, in amazement.

"I was sure our lives were done," she remembered, as they wondered how they would get to her parents' house in the nearby town of Pozarane. Standing helplessly in the street they heard a voice call out "Hata." It came from a car driven by a man who had been in her school class for 12 years.

"It was a miracle," Hata said.

The family told him it would be dangerous for him to drive them anywhere, but he laughed and said "then I am going to die with you." He took them to her father's house, where they stayed until April 28, when the police came and said "give us 100,000 DM or we will kill you all."

They were given a 30 minute ultimatum and within 20 minutes the entire village of Pozarane started walking toward the Macedonian border. After walking 200 km they were picked up by a Serbian bus that dropped them off five kilometers from the border, taking everything from them – money, documents and drivers' licenses. Some of the people were beaten, or worse. They continued toward Macedonia on foot.

They arrived there at approximately 8 PM but did not cross the border until 4 AM. During the waiting period Serbian soldiers would not allow them to accept the food and water offered by international aid groups. There was the report of a man pushing his father's wheelchair toward the border.

"You don't need him," a soldier had said, and shot the old man.

It was April 29, 1999. After staying a few nights in a hotel they were directed toward the UNHCR tent city, Stankovac 2, where they lived for three months.

Life in the camp was cold and wet but conditions were tolerable. Hata and Xhela, with their three boys and her youngest brother (who at the last minute decided not to leave the camp), signed up for migration to the United States under the recently established refugee relocation allotment. Their plane was one of the last to leave for the United States. Their next stop was to be the little red farm house on my property in Michigan City, Indiana.

For me they were a surrogate for Henkelinda and her family, from whom I kept their presence a secret. I didn't want the girl to think that she had been replaced in my heart although, of course, I wasn't sure that was not true. So, right after Hata and her family arrived, I went to find out.

In my last conversation with Henkelinda, on May 24th, they had been in Dortmund, Germany, and I was unsure what their present circumstances were, much less how the miracle of arriving in Germany had occurred. To overcome the language problem, I'd have to see them face to face. I'd have to go to Germany. And so, on July 3rd, less than two weeks after the Mehmetis arrived in Indiana, I left one family of Kosovar refugees in America to visit another in Germany.

CHAPTER 9

SAFE IN GERMANY

We sat, all eight of us, on crumbling stone steps overhung with bushes so thick the light July rain could not penetrate. A beaming Hita held an umbrella above my head, in case a drop should find its way below. We clustered close, Henkelinda, her family and me, in wonder that we were together again, in this safe, idyllic place, the Cloister Blankenburg.

How glorious had been the getting there, at least for me! The excitement of air travel, which had begun to sink into the commonplace, had now been ratcheted up a notch by the attention to minutia at an airport's security barrier. The capture of a corkscrew and nail clippers, and the dumping out of grapefruit juice as I passed through the barrier gave a heightened sense of importance to the trip. Walking down the long corridor to the plane, uniformed men and women with little beagle-type dogs sniffed at our ankles. One of these little mutts sniffed too enthusiastically at the fanny-pack of the black boy in front of me; he was asked to step aside. The same dog then went after my shoes: "I carry around the smells of a dog and cats and goats" I said. The woman laughed "you have goats!" and passed on to the man behind. I looked for the black boy later on the flight and never saw him. An older white woman, I have come to expect the privilege of such passes on my trips.

The direct Lufthansa flight from Chicago to Frankfurt had been sweetened by the anticipation of seeing Henkelinda, and I could not sleep for the excitement of it all. The moon was just past full. The plane reflected its light onto the floor of thick white clouds and it traveled as a silver shadow, following our path below. In all my fantasies a missile shoots up through that heavy white carpet, a black thrust bursting toward us, only time to gasp before it demolishes the plane, but such a missile did not materialize that night. They never do, in fact, but it doesn't spare me the fearful fantasies. Inside was near silence, all the chairs tipped back, the lights dimmed, the drone of the engines and a little tinkle from the gallery, stewardesses wandering up and down with bottles of water. A few lights stayed on, a few sleepless faces, along with mine, stared wide-eyed into the darkness. The rustle in the galley grew louder and then, without notice, the cabin lights came on, to coffee, croissants and arrival.

After a short walk in Frankfurt's slick modern airport I got a train to Hanover and dozed during the dash northward through central Germany. In Hanover, whose construction-choked station was anything but slick, it was a short wait for a train to Bremen. I was almost there. It was late afternoon and I'd been awake for 30 hours when I disembarked at Bremen. I walked across the broad plaza fronting the station, turned left and came upon a lovely small hotel, the Bremer Haus. I called Henkelinda on her "calls in only" cell phone and promised an early morning arrival in Oldenburg.

Mine was the perfect hotel room with a great window filling the end of the room that opened sidewise or tilted down from the top, a built-in bed surrounded by easily reached light switches, with a fluffy snow-white comforter folded neatly at its foot. In the hotel restaurant, I had the perfect meal, ending with figs, Gruyere cheese and a luscious German Reisling, followed by a blissful night deep in teak-ensconced eiderdown as a thunderstorm rumbled outside.

Morning brought a breakfast buffet piled with cheeses, breads and meats, fruit and nut laden cereals, the rich kaffee mit milch, the smiling padding serving women, and, as each guest enters, a nod and *Morgen* to those seated, and a similar *Viedersahn* on leaving. So genteel, so civilized, so German. A long way from Bosnia, a much much longer way from Hadžići. I took an early morning stroll through Bremen, whose pedestrian malls restricted the noise and exhaust fumes to the area around the station and then I left, suitcase in hand, to find the train to Oldenburg.

It stopped at every little town, with passengers traveling short distances – on here, off two stops later, chattering incessantly, a kind of moving social hour. Although it was already scorching hot, seven teenagers were squeezed into the seats across the aisle, laughing and hitting each other with plastic Star Wars characters, making me even hotter. A beautiful blonde conductor gave me an 'all is forgiven' smile when she saw that I had failed to get my ticket punched on the platform. Although I sat on the shaded northern side, hot air hit me through the open windows as the train whoooshed along the tracks.

As we neared Oldenburg, muscles tightened in my stomach and my throat dried up. I wondered if I would recognize her, the refugee girl that I had seen but twice, and then six months before. I gathered my things and stood, as the train slowed, in the aisle by the door, stooping slightly to survey the people on the platform as I inched gradually toward the door. I spotted her instantly, her smooth skin frozen in a frown, her eyes intent upon the door. She stood with two girls her own age, – the clunky shoes, the tousled hair, the jeans and loose fitting shirts identical, and in a flash of dismay I saw she was, as those silly ones had been across the aisle, a teenager. She was transformed into that parody of maturity that teenagers find so interesting in other teenagers, but I do not. She was no longer special, unique, out of the ordinary. My Henkelinda had joined the normal world!

This sense of Henkelinda as a typical teenaged girl, the condition I had wanted most for her, came and went during the next few days and eventually disintegrated in the onslaught of her own unique personality, but my flashbacks to that vision on the platform came back to haunt me when we were not together.

There was no failure to recognize – I could have found her in a million-person crowd. When I finally stepped onto the platform her solemn brooding face came to life, eyes brightened, smile widened, lips pulled the whole face into lively motion. We hugged and held each other a long time, flesh pressed against warm flesh, and saying goodbye to her friends, we left the station arm in arm. She had a special way of talking, lots of giggles and shakes of the head and although her English was still abominable – that which seemed so good in the camp was totally inadequate now – somehow communication was possible in person that had not been so by phone.

Passing a hotel on the little river, I went inside and registered. Henkelinda went upstairs with me, checked the television, tested the beds, inspected the bathroom and examined the view from the window in the time it took me to set my things about the room. We left and joined Nimi in the town – he had been buying groceries and was loaded down with bags – and took a taxi out through the orderly German countryside to the sylvan setting that had once housed a community of nuns. The neat brick buildings were ordered by pretty shaded sidewalks and narrow streets. Passing through the gate I was asked to show my passport, which I had left in the room.

"You cannot enter," I was told.

"But I am an American," I answered, out of my long experience of seeing it work wonders, particularly so recently in Bosnia. But the Germans, whose cultural tap root had depth and stamina that mine did not, were not so easily impressed.

"Verboten, bitte," I was told, "bitte" being that gentle universal word that so softens all expression that it's hard to imagine that it was in the Nazi vocabulary. Having traveled so far, I could not go the final 500 yards to the family's rooms. And so they came to me.

"We will have a picnic," called Henkelinda, returning with her family close behind, carrying bags and bottles in their arms. They all glowed with good spirits and good health. The skinny rag-tag kids who nine months before had squatted silently in their tent, looked strong and healthy as they hugged and pressed against me. Gufim threw chubby arms around my neck and left damp patches on my cheeks from slobbery kisses. While Dyke still spoke in sighs, they were softened by her smiles. She had a dimple I had not seen before.

I stared at Nare, at her glowing dark eyes and shining hair.

"Nare, you are beautiful!"

"Thank you," she beamed. She understood English? In all those dreary Hadžići days she had not spoken a word to me or hinted that she understood.

"Is Jecki here with you?" I asked.

"He is in Switzerland," she said. "He used to call a lot but now not so much. I do not care."

Her look told me that this was true.

Then came the sprinkle of rain that drove us into the huddle on the steps.

"Tell me everything!" I begged Henkelinda.

"Let's do our picnic first," she said.

The sun peeked out from a cloud and mist rose from the tidy well-trimmed German countryside. We walked across the field to a lake and dragged a picnic table into the shade of overhanging trees. Nare laid out feta cheese, tomatoes, cucumbers and rolls and as we ate, Henkelinda told their story. Nare and Dyke, sprawled on the opposite bench, hung eagerly on Henkelinda's words. Hita sat at my side drinking orange soda, while her sister and two brothers played close by on the grass.

"Five days on a minibus to get to Germany, they told us!"

But by March 12, when they finally left the camp, the minibus had become a truck and they crouched in the back beneath a tarp. The promised passports never materialized.

Leaving Sarajevo, they passed through that part of Bosnia controlled by unfriendly Serbs. Four times the family left the truck to walk in woods. They slept in the truck or on the ground.

The first international border was between Bosnia-Herzegovina and Croatia. They left the road and walked from 9 PM to 3 AM, with Jecki carrying Gufim. They rode the truck again until, exhausted, they arrived at a private house in Zagreb. Two days later Croatian police burst in and took them to Jakova, a Zagreb refugee camp. Henkelinda had first called me from this camp.

On the next leg, from Zagreb to Slovenia, they were again hidden in the back of a truck. At the border the truck was searched by Slovenian police. The children climbed out.

"'What is your name?' they asked Henkelinda. She told them and they sent the family back. On their second try they asked her name again, but on the third try they didn't bother.

"It's Henkelinda again," they said.

The family refused to get into the truck a fourth time and their guide Rasim proposed another plan. He took them to a spot from where, at night, they walked four hours and waded across the fast-flowing Sava River. Jecki made three trips for the little ones. Soaked and freezing, they spent the next day hidden in the truck.

"It was terrible, we did not eat, we could not leave," said Henkelinda.

Finally they were taken to a house in Ljubljana where now it was the Slovenian police who sent them to a refugee camp.

"I was angry and refused to go," said Henkelinda. "They say I have a big mouth, that I am a problem. They take me and Jecki in handcuffs to the jail. Can you imagine, putting a seventeen-year old girl in jail?"

The rest of the family were taken to the Harsnika Camp in Ljubljana. Henkelinda spent five days in a cell with other Kosovar women. Jecki was locked up longer. After they were together again in Harsnika, Rasim appeared.

"Tonight to Italy."

Two cars took them to the edge of Trieste where, one block from the border crossing, they were stopped by the Italian police. The exhausted mother fainted and was taken to a hospital. The rest of the family was driven to Harsnika, Jecki in handcuffs. After Dyke got out of the hospital Rasim came again to take them across the border. Again they were stopped and returned to Harsnika. On the third try the police took them closer, to Koper.

"Then I got sick," said Henkelinda.

"How sick?" I asked.

"Oh, I do not know the words, how can I say?" she cried. Then she bent to pick up pebbles from the ground.

"What are these?"

"Stones?"

"I got stones."

"Kidney stones!" I cried, remembering Joseph's pronouncement on the subject, as she, her sister and her mother laughed with the pleasure of my understanding.

The younger ones had gotten bored with the story-telling and stripped to their underpants, they splashed in the shallows of the lake. They gaped and we stopped our talk to watch as a pair of German scuba divers, glistening in their high-tech black and yellow wetsuits, large tanks mounted on their backs, walked into the water and disappeared below the surface. Henkelinda continued.

"I got eight infusions here . . . three here," she jabbed at her upper arm and then her finger. "But I didn't understand what was happening. No one told me nothing."

While Henkelinda was in the hospital, Jecki and Nare met the Bosnian wife of an Italian who offered to take them across the border in her little car, for 3,000 DM.

"This woman, Rosanne, is drinking all the time – wine, vodka, whiskey, everything. She drove like crazy."

On the first run she stuffed Nare and Jecki into the tiny space behind the back seat of her car and made it across the border to a refugee camp in Trieste.

"Mama came and told me Nare and Jecki were in Italy and that Nimi, Hita and Nika were going that night. And I am in hospital!" said Henkelinda.

The next day her mother came to say the three little ones had made it safely. She and Gufim would go that night. The doctor visited Henkelinda that afternoon to tell her he was operating in the morning.

"Just like that he tells me. I have nothing to say! When he is gone, I put on my clothes and leave."

Dyke and Gufim made it to Trieste, but when Rosanne tried to take Henkelinda across the border to Italy, they were caught – twice.

"Nobody else is stopped but I am caught two times! When the drinking lady came back I wouldn't go again."

"No more problems," Rosanne promised.

"'How do I know that?' I asked."

"I have paid the guards," said Rosanne.

Henkelinda finally agreed and this time it worked. On May 15, two months after they had left Sarajevo, they were all in Western Europe. A man offered to take them to Germany for 5,000 DM.

"I said it was too much. I only had 2,000 DM left. He said 4,000 and I said okay, 2,000 now and 2,000 when we get there. Then I gave him everything we had."

They went by minibus, from Italy to Austria and from Austria to Germany, crossing the borders with ease. By May 19 they were in Stuttgart and the driver demanded his 2,000 DM.

"I said we have no more money and he was very angry. He says I am a bad girl, and calls us all the time, asking for the money."

Upon their arrival in Stuttgart they reported to the German authorities, filed for asylum and were sent to the Dortmund refugee camp. Two weeks later they were moved to Oldenburg.

"Tomorrow you must come back with your passport," Henkelinda said, "and see where we live."

By now the little ones had stopped their swimming and put on their clothes. They were restless, wanting to go home. The sun was low and the air cool. A family of swans waddled up from the water and we tossed them the remains of our meal.

I called a taxi and Henkelinda rode back with me to town. In my room she lounged back on the bed, watching the German equivalent of MTV, reminding me again of her transformation into an ordinary teenager. This girl, who had been imprisoned, forded rivers, walked out of a hospital to avoid surgery, been jammed into the crevices of a little car to pass police barricades, sassed the police in Slovenia, and probably much more, adjusted quickly to the everyday world.

The next day I returned to Blankenburg, this time with my passport, and joined them in the large room that now served as home. Strewn with beds, chairs, a table, and cabinets, it was warm and sunny, adjacent to a pleasant park. Neighboring families, some of whom I met, were friendly and well spoken. It was comfortable, as were they. We spend the day in conversation and walks. Then Hita performed for me.

Hita's energy level was higher than the rest, she attended to all the spoken words, most of which she could not understand. She watched me intently and was never far away. If I should catch her eye, her responding grin was fast and bright. She had done this recitation at a gathering of displaced Kosovars, I was told, and brought tears to everyone's eyes. She stood in the center of the room, straight and sturdy, and began to orate, in a strong emotion-packed voice, words I could not understand. But, by her flamboyant gestures, the brilliance of her eyes, the phrases that she sang to the corners of the room, it had an impact of its own, it spoke of suffering, despair and finally, of triumph and victory. I wrote down the words in Albanian and had them translated, later, by Alban Mehmeti, who spoke the best English in his own family, as follows:

I swear, I swear, we are Albanians
I'll never cut my long hair
I will win my Republic
I won my Republic
For one year in the war I stayed
One mother and six children in the woods
Into every home and in every mountain
We were without our father
Our uncle saved our life
As a dragon in the woods of Kleges
My uncle is back in Deçan fighting
His name is Mehmet Osaj.

It was so simple. A little nationalism, some defiance, a few lines giving their sad story and homage to their wonderful uncle, Dyke's brother, "A dragon in the woods . . . Mehmet Osaj." It was actually more powerful when I didn't understand what it meant, by Hita's rendering, but I wondered about this

Mehmet Osaj, picturing him as a fierce, mustached and powerful freedom fighter for the KLA. I also wondered about the missing father, as I had many times before.

When I had first asked about the father, I had been told they didn't know where he was, and they were reticent to say more. I interpreted this as meaning that he had disappeared into the ranks of the KLA. I had an image of him holed up in the woods, fighting to the death, shoulder to shoulder with this dragon, Mehmet Osaj. My idea of the KLA was fashioned, perhaps, by pictures I had seen at the time of Rambouillet, of Hasim Thaqi, a large, powerful, handsome man, with the look of determination and no small measure of defiance on his face. I saw the father of these beautiful children as much like that.

I asked again, as we sat together this summer afternoon, if they had news of their father yet, and got back a terse, evasive "no." Again, I was hesitant to pry.

The German government was moving them, the next day, to their own apartment many miles away.

"We are going to Peine," they said, but they would actually be in the tiny suburb of Edemeissen. It would take several days to move them, so I said I'd meet them there, in two days.

"How will you find us," asked Henkelinda.

"It can't be too hard," I said, assuming that there would be a settlement of refugees from Kosovo there, and so I took a train the following morning to Berlin, a city I had never visited, to fill the time while they were being moved, to satisfy a longtime interest of my own. But I had no map and missed the stop in West Berlin, disembarking in East Berlin instead. At street level there was nothing but industrial buildings and a dreary café. I went back to the platform and inquired. They sent me back the way I came.

West Berlin, at the Zoo stop, was another world. I dropped my things at a hotel and for a day and a half, hiked the town, took a walking tour of the old Wall, visited Checkpoint Charlie, sauntered down der Linden and tried to imagine the Berlin of old movies – unsuccessfully – in this modern place. The remnants of the past lay mostly in ruins, new construction was everywhere. The Berlin of my dreams (and movies) was long gone.

I took the train to Peine the following day and asked a taxi to take me to Edemeissen. The driver spoke English and I told him I wanted to go to the "refugee camp". He had no idea what I meant. We went instead to the town hall where I went from office to office unsuccessfully inquiring – everyone was very polite – as to where a refugee family might be situated. By accident I was overheard by a woman.

"That might be the family Heinrich is moving in," she said, and when we went to the address she had suggested, there was my family, along with

Heinrich, the social worker, settling in. I'd found my needle in the German haystack, one of the many miracles that marked my serendipitous acquaintance with this family.

German and American approaches to refugees are quite different. We allow in very few but let them stay. The Germans, on the other hand, open their arms generously to people in distress, yet when distress is over, the country sends them back. The Mehmetis would be eligible for U.S. citizenship in five years; Henkelinda's family would be sent home from Germany as soon as Kosovo was inhabitable. While Hata and Xhela were expected to get jobs, back home, German refugees were not allowed to work. In both countries, happily, the children are well taken care of, accepted into the schools. Heinrich and his agency had furnished this house – two comfortable rooms, a kitchen and living room – with all the necessities including a television and a telephone. Across the courtyard was another large and rambling room equipped with many beds, for sleeping. Both places had heat and electricity and were equipped with bathrooms. No luxuries here, but privacy. This place was their own.

Henkelinda took the bus with me back to Peine, where I found my own more than comfortable room at the Schützenhaus Hotel, up a dark (until I discovered the light button with the tiny red eye), narrow staircase at the side of the bar, a room big enough only for the single bed, long desk and a little wardrobe, it had a narrow shower in the bath, double-opening window, and a TV with no English channels; from my built in bed I could touch every other piece of furniture, one of those cozy perfectly fitted German rooms I love so much, of scrubbed blond wood with a pure white pile of pillows and featherbed on the bed, a perfect reading light, an ersatz womb. My window opened onto the parking lot and I can tell you the exact closing hour of the bar below, but other than that, pure silence was Peine. At breakfast I was greeted by cereal, eggs, rolls, juice and a wooden board with meats and cheese, decorated with a big spring of parsley; three other (German) guests were eating; there were ten rooms in total, at 95 DM each. Peine did not have a large tourist trade.

I spent the next two days with the family. We went for pizza or ate pita in their kitchen – pita being meat or cheese filled puff pastry, not the more familiar rounds of unleavened bread of that same name. Then I left for home. One week was all I could spare from the Mehmetis and the farm. But I had not told Henkelinda about the Mehmetis – I felt like a bigamist who justified her guilty secret as a kindness to the betrayed party.

By now NATO bombing had driven the Serbian army from Kosovo and many ethnic Albanians were beginning to return. A KFORS had been established, much like the SFORS in Sarajevo, to keep the peace.

"Will they send you home soon?" I asked.

"Perhaps. We are afraid."

"You don't want to go home?"

"There is nothing for us there – it is all gone."

Their journey was not over, but for now they were safe, well-fed and warm at night, and all the children were in school. We were beginning to live in the same world.

"When will you come to see us again?" asked Henkelinda, the last morning.

"Soon, and maybe you will be in Kosovo. You can be sure, when they send you back, that I will come and visit there."

We both expected it to be the following spring.

CHAPTER 10

JUST MERELY PRESENT

I saw them many times again, never in Kosovo. On one trip, in November, 2000, I impulsively changed travel plans, at Amsterdam's Schiphol Airport, to complete some unfinished business before I visited Henkelinda and her family. I heaved my pack onto my back and took a train to The Hague to visit the International Criminal Tribunal for the Former Yugoslavia (ICTY), where trials were underway for crimes perpetrated during the war in Bosnia, although most people had little hope for justice from this international court. I had no idea who was currently on trial but it felt important, even necessary, to attend. There was too much horror in the Balkan histories of my new friends that I didn't understand.

Trains for *Den Haag* leave regularly from the airport and in less than an hour I was in the seat of Holland's government, an old fashioned, intimate town. My first hours there bode poorly for this change of plans. At the station a friendly young girl gave directions: first to the Bel Air Hotel, which she said was close to the Peace Palace and then to the Palace itself, where she claimed the trials were taking place.

"An easy walk," she assured me.

After an hour's hike, pack on my back, in a chilly rain, I reached the hotel. Checking in but not daring to lie down for fear of falling asleep – I was exhausted – I went on to the imposing Peace Palace, expecting to find the seat of justice for the former Yugoslavian war criminals among its stained glass and tapestries. Not so, a guard pointed out, but he either didn't know or couldn't explain in English where I might find the trials. He wrote down a telephone number I should call. Across the street the proprietor of a tiny restaurant let me use the phone; the voice on the other end of the line told me the trials were at the Congress building. Where was the Congress building? The restaurant owner gave me directions, right back to my hotel. The Congress building, a hunched down grey two storied affair, was just next door.

It was an unlikely setting for confronting genocide. The only hint of global goings-on inside was the robin's egg blue United Nations flag that fluttered peacefully in front. Inside the security booth one apple-cheeked young soldier poked at the contents of my purse, another put my camera in a locker, unlocked the door and waved me through; my pink visitor's pass was number 9136. No passport check, no caring if I had business there or what it might be – a momentous moment for me but not for anyone else. I stepped inside and faced an empty lobby, cold, marble and still, absent the expected celestial roar.

At least there was a security check. The metal detector beeped as I walked through, startling me far more than it reasonably should have, and I returned to place my tinny necklace in the pass-through tray. Retrieving it and my equilibrium, I climbed one of two curving staircases to *Trial Chamber I*, picked up a set of earphones from the table outside and nervously stepped into a low ceilinged room where two guards lazed against the wall. Rows of dentist-office chairs of blue and chrome faced a glass partition. Someone, somewhere, was whistling *Deck the Halls*.

The 100-seat room was empty but for two couples, an artist with his easel propped before him and a tailored woman near whom I settled. I had expected an angry snarling mob. A few young people whispered among themselves in the section marked *Press*. Before us was what would have been an ordinary courtroom scene, had it not been staged behind a thick glass wall. Three judges looked down from their dais: the stately Portuguese chief justice, a dark-skinned somber Egyptian and a chubby little American woman, Patricia Wald. The prosecution filled the right hand side, two rows of men and women at desks, headphones in place, busy at something I didn't comprehend. A single left side row of men represented the defense and at center stage a recorder sat and bailiff stood, both gowned in black with pleated white bibs. Facing them all, his back to us, his meager audience, was the defendant. The events of the morning dropped away, along with my fatigue. In this orderly lackluster setting, my heart pounded as if to break. The defendant was Radislav Krstić. The subject was Srebrenica.

It was already five years since the Bosnian Serb Army (VRS) had marched those seven thousand men from Srebrenica off to their deaths after which the few survivors reported the gleeful gunning down of most of those unarmed Bosnians. The court's six-count indictment charged this defendant with these murders, genocide, extermination and persecutions, arguing that they occurred "under command and control of Radislav Krstić and Ratko Mladić." I well knew the name of Mladić, responsible for countless monstrous deeds in both Bosnia in Kosovo. But who was Radislav Krstić?

Leaving his chair to examine a map, Krstić turned his face. I scarcely dared to look and when I did, was stunned at what I saw.

"Bob Johnson!"

It was not, of course, the kind and gentle Chicagoan of my acquaintance, but the two men shared some common physical traits. My shock was that the likeness was of a decent-looking, modest man. I should not have been surprised. Hannah Arendt, after all, had told us forty years before that the new and banal face of evil, Adolph Eichmann's in Jerusalem, was "terribly and terrifyingly normal." Color this monster-man not satanic black nor homicidal red, but Babbitt grey. His lawyer, Nenad Petrušić looked to be the violent one with his fierce frowning features and a chock of black hair swept back from his rocky face. Krstić's greying hairline receded to the back of his scalp, leaving behind a scattering of fuzzy wisps. He wore a baggy dark grey suit and his white collar rose up stiffly about his flaccid neck as if both ill-fitting items had been pulled from a rarely opened closet, much as my farmer uncle's had on those infrequent occasions when he went to church. The *Teddy Kennedy* reading glasses perched on his nose gave him a clerkish look.

The prosecuting attorney, black-gowned Peter McCloskey, an older, balding Kevin Spacey, was cross-examining Krstić in this ninth month of the trial. Formal and deferential, he questioned the accused about a map which, although it faced the opposite way, I followed on a ceiling monitor. He asked the defendant to identify features within the UN-protected area encompassing Srebrenica.

McCloskey made his inquiries in patient respectful tones. Krstić answered slowly, carefully. The judges asked questions to clarify. All this in French, English and BCS (Bosnian/ Croatian/ Serbian, a single language which, for political reasons, was now defined as three). The judges called for a break and when court reconvened, only I and the other lone woman remained.

"Where are you from?" I asked.

"It's, uh, difficult . . ." she stammered.

"I'm sorry I asked," I said, realizing, to my horror, that Krstić might have a wife and if he did, this might be she.

The translation of choice squawked through our headphones with McCloskey questioning:

"Were you aware that the 25,000 in Srebrenica, a city that had held a population of 8,000 before the siege, were lacking medical aid, housing, water, food and electricity?"

"I knew nothing about that. It was under the jurisdiction of someone else."

"Were you aware that those people were starving to death?"

"I really didn't know."

Krstić's argument appeared to be the classic one – that he was doing his job, the military task of separating Srebrenica from another safe area, Žepa. He laid the blame for overrunning Srebrenica on Mladić, who took command before the nasty work began.

"When exactly was that?" the prosecutor asked.

"Before noon on the 10ᵗʰ," claimed the defendant in our English translation. "We [another commander and himself] were just merely present."

Just merely present as, the following day, the VRS overran the UN posts and crashed into the town, guns blasting; *just merely present*, as they drove helpless civilians from their homes, *just merely present* as 7,000 men were marched off to their deaths.

The details of David Rohde's book came streaming back. I remembered that NATO planes circled minutes away, poised to deliver the missiles that would have insured that the UN "safe area" was truly safe, that UN officials in Zagreb refused them that opportunity but this was a different perspective. This man was on the other, the brutally successful side.

It was an irony for this court, at this moment, to be in Holland, home of those UN representatives who had played such a critical role in the massacre that followed. Not only the soldiers who failed, inevitably, the task of preserving the safety of that town, nor even their Secretary of Defense who worried more about his thirty men than the 25,000 inhabitants of the town. The most shame lay with the Dutch commander being bullied into lifting his glass to Mladić for a photo op. Was Krstić standing nearby? And had he been chuckling at how clever they all had been? And at what fools peopled the other side? If Krstić recognized the irony, he was unlikely to feel good about it now.

I thought of Mina, whom I had met in Sarajevo, who had survived Srebrenica and was struggling to repair her shattered life. I could not have imagined then, as I felt her pain ricochet about in my own brain, that such evil could be punished by something as prosaic as this trial. I was wrong. I was beginning to see that this highly civilized proceeding was the only way to go. If she had been given the job of handing out justice to this man, he would not have survived an hour, nor should we expect otherwise. Better that McCloskey and the others, speaking and acting out of impersonal objectivity, be given the job.

I sat through two sessions of the ICTY tribunal and found some comfort in its very tedium. That's what *due process* is, the quiet, contemplative, highly proscribed environment in which judgments are made and truth is sought with all the imperfections of our well-intended humanity. It is the best we've got and far better than those judgments made when blood is boiling and hearts are ruling minds. This man was being given a chance to defend himself, one that he deserved far less than those Srebrenica thousands to whom it was denied. Within the quagmire of our shame are tiny flecks of pride. The court plods on and may someday catch up with the events it tracks. Justice is not a speedy thing but we ask it to be sturdy and stay the course. And in this courtroom, so it did.

Judgment would not be rendered for Mr. Krstić for another year, nor sentencing for another five. By then another prisoner had joined him at the Hague – Slobodan Milosevic, removed in a flash from the technicolor nightly news to the dull grey hues of confinement. That's where he ought to be. I wouldn't have known this if I had not gone to – been present at – The Hague. Presence is everything in life: understanding, commitment, complicity, to name a few. It is an oxymoron to be just merely present. Krstić had not been – nor was I.

One night at the Bel Aire Hotel and two days in the courtroom next door were monumental for me. Being there gave first hand depth and meaning to the ugliness to which I'd been a second-hand witness, both in Bosnia and Kosovo. I was not at Srebrenica but I was at one small piece of the vitally important aftermath. I had been truly present.

I left the Hague and went on to Edemeissen.

CHAPTER 11

NEXT STEPS

I went back to Edemeissen the next year, the next, the next, the next and for the last time, in 2005. The first two times I had, as in Bosnia, a total disconnect, leaving my world for theirs, then back again. In Frankfort Airport I would walk to the train station and head north, changing in Hanover for the Berlin train that stopped at Peine, where Henkelinda would meet me. We traveled on to Edmeissen by bus.

The children were in school and doing well. They were learning German fast, bringing home grades to make their mother proud and more than holding their own in sports. Nimi, now in his teens, missed the opportunity to travel with his soccer team to Spain, although he was a valued player. Refugees, having no passports, could not leave Germany. I watched him play and later watched Hita, in a gymnasium where she was a scoring star and clearly the favorite of her coach. Donika, the quiet one, was number one in academics.

Nare, too old for school, stayed with her mother in the apartment since, as a refugee, she could not work in Germany. Back in the United States Hata and Xhela were looking desperately for work and while they benefited from food stamps and Medicaid, those benefits would dwindle rapidly and without the quantities of assistance from The Group they'd be quite destitute.

This family, on the other hand, were generously provided with housing, food and a living allowance, were not allowed to take a job from a German worker, and would be shipped back to their home country as soon as feasible. But although Kosovo was calm enough, after the first year Dyke's poor health kept the German Government from sending them home.

Not that the authorities hadn't tried. On my second trip to Edemeissen I went with Henkelinda to the offices of the "sociale," the social worker that oversaw their life in Germany. By the frozen smile on his face when we sat down I knew that he was no fan of Henkelinda's. His look brought back to me a memory of the Slovenian soldier's words of disgust as he lifted the tarp in the back of the truck: "Henkelinda again!"

The family had already made a fool of this man and he knew who the gang leader was. Scheduled to join other refugees on a return flight to their native country, they had been ordered to be prepared for a police pickup. But when the police arrived at the appointed time the family was visiting an aunt in Dusseldorf and soon after that they secured a court order keeping them in Germany until a scheduled hearing before a judge. That hearing had come and gone with the judge allowing them to stay because of Dyke's high blood pressure and poor health, and so the plans of "sociale" had been thwarted by this girl.

Nor was the German social worker beyond prejudices. When I argued the sorry conditions in Kosovo, including remnants of the fighting between Serbian and Albanian speakers, Henkelinda pointed her finger into the air in playful representation of a gun.

"These people are consumed with violence," said Herr Dietrich. A German said this, yet.

She knew how to avoid what she didn't want, but she was not at all sure how to get what she wanted, and I suspected that she wasn't even sure what that might be. What I wanted for her was a first rate education that would lead to a career. It was much more likely that she had no expectations beyond the family's present, relatively satisfactory situation. She was finishing her courses at the local school, and had no place to continue, in work or study, under the terms of German refugee law. She and I went together to meet with a former teacher.

"Doesn't she have any way to stay in school?" I asked.

"Of course she does – but she will have to travel to Braunsweig," Ms. Schroeder said, "and it is hard to get into that school."

The German education system with its different tracks for different folks was a labyrinth I struggled to understand. We tried phone calls and made office visits. I had enough hutzpah to make up for her shyness in this strange new situation; I could open doors that she could not. After I left she struggled on her own until it was settled that she would travel daily by train to Braunsweig to continue her studies.

Back in the camp the other children had been no more than shadows behind Henkelinda, five refugee children among scores, but in Germany they moved into the foreground. Report cards, bicycles, squabbling, junk food, watching Babar and Bruce Willis on TV, homework, were of a kind with my grandchildren at home and I genuinely enjoyed their company. One afternoon, lying on the floor with Nimi, Hita and Donika, playing language games to test how much we could communicate, we laughed more than we spoke.

I never made that kind of connection with Nare (too old?) or Gufim (too young?), and I was always uncomfortable with Dyke. On each of my trips I slipped her small amounts of cash and she grasped my hand in hers and called me an angel but this gentle soul had none of her children's vibrancy. She was in a perpetual – as my Aunt Bertha would have phrased it – sinking spell. It was Henkelinda who remained my solid friend, my main link to the others. I was charmed by her ebullient openness – her emotions came gushing out with enough force to keep the meagerness of her English words afloat. Except on one subject, where she continued to lie to me: her father.

In the refugee camp she told me the father – Ali by name – had disappeared, and I did not pursue the subject, thinking that he might be among the desperate fighters in the mountains, perhaps already dead. But when I raised the question later, she said he was in Albania, trying to come to Germany. It all seemed rather vague. Back home, Hata had quickly straightened me out.

"He's walked out on the family, gone with another woman," she had said.

"How can you possibly know that?" I asked.

"It's done all the time in Kosovo. When the man walks out, as happens frequently, the family is too ashamed to admit it. The man is king there and without a man a woman is nothing. I'm sure that's the case with your Henkelinda."

So on our first bus trip from Peine to Edemeissen I said "tell me the truth about your father." To my surprise, she did.

"He is in Berlin, with another woman," she said.

"Berlin!"

"Yes, but I have taken care of that," she added, explaining that several boys in her class had driven her to Berlin. They went to her father's place and she confronted the woman who opened the door.

"Do you know you are living with the father of six children?" asked Henkelinda. The details of the encounter, as with most of Henkelinda's stories, were vague, but the woman had cleared out and Ali had come to visit his family in Edemeissen.

"He is going to come to live with us," Henkelinda added, "when he gets his papers straightened out." I did not believe it.

On my next trip to Edemeissen, however, Ali was there. A little dump of a man, he sat quietly on the wide curving sofa, that first afternoon, as the little ones chattered in their few words of English and Henkelinda and I carried on a conversation that included, through her translation, most of them. I had no interest in – no use for – him. They are more my family now, I thought, than yours. I added to myself, truth be known, an uncomplimentary epithet.

Later Ali was sent back to Kosovo while they remained in Germany and soon after he arrived there I got a call from Henkelinda with a request that she had never made before – for money. To help her father set up a home for them when they returned, she said.

"No." I said. "When you return I will try to help you but I will not help your father."

She did not argue and never brought it up again. He had put her up to it, I guessed, and among her better traits was filial loyalty. She knew better than I did, no doubt, that any money sent would be used for purposes other than to bring his family back to his bosom.

The subject having surfaced on that first bus ride, I quickly learned more. Ali's troubles began as long ago as 1991, when he was manager in a textile factory in nearby Jakova, where they then lived. Milosevic was beginning to put the squeeze on Albanians and the Serbian police were already on the lookout for agitators. They asked Ali to tell them things, give names – Henkelinda wasn't sure exactly what – and when he refused, they put him in jail. When he was out "on bail" the family escaped the country for Sweden where they lived as refugees, going to good schools and learning Swedish, but as is the case for refugees in most European countries, they were asked to return home less than two years later. Their home in Jacova had been taken over by the Serbs, so they moved into a house near Ali's family, in Strelc. But Ali continued to be of great interest to the police and he left for Germany in 1995, this time alone, to escape more harassment from the police. It was during their earlier stay in Sweden that they had met the couple we had called from Sarajevo.

On my second visit to Germany I took a room in Edemeissen at a B & B within walking distance of the apartment. The Hofhansen Gastezimmer had four rooms and a little breakfast room on the second floor. My room was tiny and I shared a bath but curled in bed at night with a good reading light and an even better book, it was utter comfort. With the family just down the street, I had longer and more dreamless sleeps than I ever had at home. And in the morning, at whatever hour I specified the night before, the breakfast table would be laid in elegant blue and white china surrounded by a tray of cheese and meat, little pots of jam, honey and chocolate, rolls and brown bread, mango juice, homemade sausages and a pot of hot coffee. I never saw another guest, although I sometimes heard them in the hall.

I didn't see Ali after that first day, neither on that trip nor any other. He may not have enjoyed my company.

My next trip to Edemeissen closed the gap between my two worlds. I was traveling with my son, his wife and their one-year old daughter Paige. We had rented a little vacation cottage in Holland and were off to see the European sights, in this case Berlin. Henkelinda was an important stop on route, far more important to me than to the others, because I needed to pull these two parts of my life together. It was high time! We spent two warm sunny days with them, quite happily. Dyke and Nare cooked an Albanian feast; Paige played with the younger kids while my daughter-in-law Deborah lay on the grass with Nare, giving her advice to mend her love-torn heart. This most mysterious of the six children had, since my last visit, run away, married, had the marriage annulled and returned home. The details baffled me and frankly, I didn't care to understand, but somehow in Deb's first trip overseas she proved herself an adept marriage counselor to a non–English speaking young woman. I was impressed. My son John threw and kicked balls with the younger ones, repaired a bike, pulled carts and made himself the hit with kids he always was. While Henkelinda and I sat and talked, Dyke listened to us, smiling and nodding, though I doubted she understood a word.

Paige with Nika, Hita, Nimi and Gufim

It was more than a year later that I next visited. I slept in the cozy Hofstader once again; this time I had the one room with a private bath, pure luxury. At Henkelinda's it was a different kind of scene and I didn't look forward as eagerly to joining them mornings. There was a young man, Izmet, courting Henkelinda and causing great distress to the rest of the family. His name could not be mentioned without teasing from the younger children, complaints from Dyke and sarcastic jibes from Nare. It all baffled me, particularly the attitude of Nare, who I would have thought, considering her own romantic interlude, might be sympathetic. Izmet, a Kosovar who had been in Germany as a worker and held a German passport, had met Henkelinda in Braunsweig, where she had finally gotten a room week days, while she attended school. As a result of this new liaison, Dyke insisted that she give up the room and travel home each night, a grueling schedule, since it included not only the train to and from Peine but a bus to Edemeissen as well, at both ends of the day. I suspected that her days as a student were numbered.

I organized a trip to the Hanover Zoo. We traveled in two cars, mine and Izmet's, and the day was full of the complexities of normal family life. Cute Gufim and sweet Donika threw tantrums because of the car they were assigned to, Nare bossed the little ones around and was nasty to Izmet, Dyke had one of her perpetual sinking spells, and she, who had illegally crossed rivers at midnight, claimed to be too terrified to get into a sightseeing boat. She then refused food until after we'd finished waiting in the long line to declare that she'd have something after all. The sturdy energetic little girls held their noses in the monkey house and refused to look at the peccary because they were related to the forbidden and hated "pork". Even my darling Henkelinda couldn't make up her mind about anything and was in constant touch by cellphone with her brother Nimi, whom she scolded incessantly in Albanian. Poor Izmet, who teased little Gufim and smooched with Henkelinda every chance he got, offered to drive Dyke home when she declared she could go no further, yet after he had made the hour long drive there and back he got only criticism from Nare who in Dyke's absence had set herself up as the matriarch.

But Hanover had a spectacular zoo, with tiger cubs, interaction with pelicans and other animals and a remarkable Indian elephant exhibit featuring a giant video of an elephant giving birth. Everyone was thrilled. When we got home exhausted, at the end of the day, we discovered that Dyke had been preparing a giant meal and then was hurt that we – particularly I – were all too full to eat. I've met this mildly manipulative mother somewhere else before, I thought. In fact I'd met them all. They were no longer exotic refugees, they were a family with ordinary foibles; they were just plain folks. I had been with them constantly for four days and it was a bit much. I retreated to my gastezimmer and took my time returning the next day.

Eventually Henkelinda left the family and moved in with Izmet in Braunsweig and when their son was born, soon after the arrival of my tenth grandchild, I went to visit, bringing a suitcase full of baby clothes that my daughters contributed. Helping Henkelinda give the infant his first bath I felt as close to her as I had to my daughter Debbie, a few weeks before, though

Debbie no longer needed my help with the bath – Joelle was her fourth! Although Henkelinda was living with Izmet and having his child, she was still not ready to marry. We are good together sometimes, she told me, and other times we are not. Something I had heard before.

Henkelinda, the bride

My last trip was right after they finally married – I couldn't make the wedding because of commitments at home, but as recompense I invited the family to a restaurant celebration. Dyke and the children came, Henkelinda and Izmet and the baby, as well as Nare and the man that she had left home to live with shortly after my last visit. The mystery of her behavior toward Henkelinda and Izmet only grew. The meal went on into the night and as the two men drank heavily of red wine and grew boisterous, Dyke sunk into one of her spells and was complaining mightily of the hour. I finally suggested that we get her home, a remark that, when translated, drew a comment in German from Nare's man that drew a laugh.

"What did he say?" I asked Henkelinda.

"That when America speaks, everyone has to do as they are told."

Hmm. Maybe my time here is done, I thought.

And so, I concluded as I flew back home, it was. The family had achieved normalcy in their adopted country, the four younger children had the advantages of one of the world's best educational systems and the two oldest girls had made what was probably the inevitable choice of being wife and mother.

My Kosovar adventure was drawing to a close, but there remained just one more place I had to go and I knew I could convince Mary to join me. We would go to Kosovo.

CHAPTER 12

KOSOVO VISIT

Landing in Pristina the landscape below looks like a Zurich or Vienna – red roofs, soft mountains blending into hills, flat seeded fields carved out of deep green woods, clusters of homes. Not like the war torn nation we had expected. Nor did I have the terrible feeling of when we first dropped down into Sarajevo. Perhaps landing in a damaged Balkan city had become old hat to me. NATO'S SFOR trucks were replaced, here on the tarmac, by their KFOR military vehicles.

Although I'd never been in Kosovo before, it felt familiar. In the passport control line, a young man turned to stare into my face.

"Nancy?"

It was Vallon, a friend of the Mehmetis whom I had met several times at their home. Mary had noticed Vallon on the plane – it is hard to overlook him, with his shockingly scared face and his sightless eye.

"He has had repeated reconstructive surgeries in the States," I said, "and is looking much better now."

"Injured in the war?" she asked.

"You could say so. It was from a mine, playing, as a boy."

We collected our baggage without mishap and stepping outdoors, where Albanians pressed against the low fence to greet arriving passengers, Val's father Esau stood, another familiar smiling face. And just beyond was the other one, the one we both had been so excited to see, Esad with his handsome toothy grin, looking less lean and hungry than before. Returning home had done him good! He had been transformed from a skinny kid in a refugee camp to a happy, successful young man. His English was serving him well – he was translating for the United Nations folks and making enough money to send most of it home to his mother in Mitrovica. German Deutschmark were the currency of Kosovo, as they were of Bosnia. He was making 1000 DM a month; his expenses were 100 for his room, 50 for electricity and he gave up to 800 DM to his mother each month.

"You will meet my mother," he said, hugging us.

The airport was adjacent to a Russian military compound. They were not treated well by the Kosovars, who remembered their alliance with Milosevic during the fighting.

"I feel sorry for those soldiers," said Esad, "they would starve if the local Serbs didn't help them."

Mary had picked the hotel, the Iliria, old and seedy, a bath with no curtain, cruddy fixtures and only drips of water from the shower. I guessed that she would soon suggest a move to the Grand Hotel, where most foreigners bedded down and where hot water was doubtlessly plentiful.

We left our things and sat with Esad at an outside table on Mother Teresa Street. Mother Teresa was Albanian, Esad points out. Who knew? Click goes the shutter, as the world gets smaller.

In my head were Hata's Pristina and Henkelinda's too, but being in this Pristina was different – neither troubled nor terrifying. It was a manageable place with a small city feeling, cars passing at normal speeds, people chatting as they meandered past. Nearby buildings appeared to be in poor repair but there was no sign, from where we sat, of NATO bombing. We drank red wine and talked, then walked, as Esad described the town. Although I had expected bombed out blocks, only three buildings had been destroyed by NATO: the telecommunications building, the old Post Office and the Serb army headquarters. We saw no other destruction except shattered glass near those targets. The most spectacular ruin in the city was the gigantic sports stadium, which had burned down after the war. There were a few modern buildings, and a large compound of UN buildings, the place where Esad provided translations and administrative assistance to the United Nations police, particularly the murder squad. One of the biggest problems they were dealing with, one that upset him very much, was prostitution. Children from Eastern Europe and Russia were being sold as sex slaves.

Esad was clearly a favorite with his international colleagues – they teased him with American nicknames – Hound Dog, Pimp Daddy. He had taken a week of vacation to be with us.

"Whatever you want, I am available," he said. Without him we could not have made this trip, we had so many things to do. Such generosity, repaying what we had done for him, in spades. So rarely does one get full payback with interest so quickly and so copiously.

After the next morning's breakfast "complete" in the Iliria, with its boiled egg and "hen pate," we paid 100 DM for our one night and walked to the Grand Hotel (220 DM per night). It had an aura of luxury, with TV, a big lobby with large soft chairs that you fell back into, a white tableclothed restaurant with a violinist and piano player and fancy new elevators. It was pretending to the westerners that frequented it that they were in their own world. But upstairs out of sight there was filthy carpet in the guest rooms and scratchy red plaid blankets folded within the sheets. We looked out to the burned out sports stadium and down on a UN compound where white trucks came and went, after passing through a monitored barrier. Just beyond was a mall of shops, restaurants and bars, from which music wafted (blasted, rather) into our room late into the night.

With Esad we took a taxi – most of them lined up in front of the Grand Hotel, where the best business was – to find the same U.S. non-governmental agency, Women for Women, that we had visited in Zagreb. We had no address, only the indication of a neighborhood and a suggestion of the kind of building the offices were in. Up and down we went, our white-haired driver stopping to inquire, unsuccessfully, along the way. His house was in this neighborhood and he stopped by to introduce us to his wife. Esad called from his cell phone to the organization and finally we found the house converted to office, hidden behind another house that fronted the road.

Eventually we three were crowded into a tiny second floor office listening to a young Kosovar woman, Hamide, telling us what she and Women for Women were doing there. She annoyed me by disregarding our questions, until I realized that, like so many we met, she was better at talking than understanding English. Her organization was training 500 women in various so-called employable skills; at least they would have been if there had been such jobs available, which there were not. Sixty percent of Kosovars were unemployed; only 300,000 working at all. Along with their military and their hard ways, the Serbians had retreated to Belgrade taking along their capital investments, management skills, economic assets, international connections and business expertise. They had cut Albanians out of the economy for most of the last decade, as factories closed, manufacturing came to a halt, resources dwindled and capital investment dried up. Women for Women was issuing a small number of micro loans through local banks; they had 423 sponsors. But Hamide was facing a special problem in Kosovo – one we had not experienced in either Zagreb or Sarajevo – the dramatically subservient role of the woman.

"We have leadership classes," she said, and then explained that she was not talking about leadership within the community. That was far too advanced for Kosovo.

"These are very elementary feminist sessions," she said, "teaching women how to stand up for their rights against their husband and husband's family, against the 'old ways.' One of our women couldn't come to a class without her seven-year old son accompanying her – he qualified as the necessary "man." The old traditions, Hamide said in disgust, prohibit a woman from appearing in public alone.

Hamide herself, born in Kosovo, had been in Pristina for less than a month. She was widely criticized for leaving her husband and children in London to take this job.

Later that afternoon we made a second stop. Mary's involvement with Women for Women had prompted her to sponsor a young Pristina woman, Rimsia. With Esad again as our translator we visited her home, where 13 people lived in two rooms: the parents, four sisters, three brothers, one sister-in-law and 3 children, aged 7, 3 and ten months. The 13 mattresses were piled to the ceiling in the kitchen.

Rimsia's family came from a farm in Podujevo, burned out during the war with Serbia. We were entertained formally in the second room, and urged to sample the apricot nectar, nuts and bananas laid out artistically before us. It was hot, the air oppressive and only Esad seemed relaxed, translating, smiling, sharing private jokes with them in Albanian, with us in English.

The difficulties of life in post-war Kosovo showed on the faces of the four beautiful sisters. They had all taken Hamide's training courses and now they sat at home doing nothing, because there were no jobs, no way to use their skills. They knitted and did embroidery. They had items on display at the crafts shop run by Women for Women – we had passed it on a back street near the old post office – but there was no one in town that had money for elegant table linens or beautifully crocheted baby blankets. Besides, most women were satisfied with the ones they made themselves. These items were for tourists, but Pristina is far from being a tourist destination. We promised to visit the shop, in hopes of finding something to buy, but we never did.

Rimsia's story was worse than that of her sisters. She had been married, but a back problem was discovered that prevented her from bearing children, according to a doctor, so her husband left her. Once married and then left, there was no possibility of another marriage. Without a husband, a Kosovar woman is nothing – we had heard it many times. Rimsia was nothing, with a difficult and painful back, to boot.

"What could be done?" asked Mary.

"A spa?" Rimsia offered hopefully.

"More usefully a doctor," answered Mary abruptly, promising to arrange for a consultation that she would attend, before we left.

Esad joined us for breakfast the next day, before we left to visit Hata's family. As we stepped out of the hotel a wave from the taxi line caught our eye. It was yesterday's driver who knew a good fare when he found one. He drove a white Mercedes that he had bought for $8000 in Germany. Many years ago he had gone there to purchase it and drive it home.

Moving south from Pristina, the road was good, with only a few pot holes, but there were no road signs and fairly heavy traffic. It clearly would be difficult to navigate this country alone, as I was to find out later.

The countryside was splattered with the signs of war – not the bombing, according to Esad, but the paramilitary ethnic cleansing by the Serbs. There were the concrete skeletons of homes everywhere – mere foundations, sometimes supporting partial walls. There were huge army vehicles everywhere, but they made us feel more secure, not less. We passed a small settlement, Kloklot, that Esad told us was entirely Serbian.

"It's loaded with KFOR," he said, "making it safe for the unpopular Serbs."

Before entering Pozuranje we were stopped by the Kosova Police Service and the driver's papers checked without a glance at us in the back seat. In the village itself there were no street signs and Esad went into a store to ask directions. He made a call and minutes later Hata's younger brother, Besniku, pulled into the parking lot in his little VW Golf. He looked familiar and I remembered that his photo had been on the refugee paperwork I had received two years before. It was he who almost joined his sister's family in America but at the last minute stayed behind, to be with his fiancee. Now they were married and had a small child.

We followed him to his father's house where everyone was gathered in our honor: Hata's elderly parents, their three sons and their wives, all of whom lived together in this spacious house, along with Hata's two sisters who drove in from their own homes to join us for the day. The house was new, with sparkling tile floors, brick walls, and large sunny rooms. It had been built since the war. Inside we gathered in a living room lined with couches, an arrangement of furniture which we had seen at Rimsia's and which defined Hata's and Xhela's home in Michigan City. There was no scattering of armchairs, side tables and throw rugs in a Kosovar room, there was a giant conversation area edged with sofas, surrounding tables upon which large amounts of food and drink were always placed.

We were offered fruit and soda and coffee and the talk, with Esad in the center, began. The talk of Hata brought tears to her mother's eyes. The talk of the boys brightened every eye. I did not speak of their many battles to adjust to their new country and the foreign language. Hata had asked me to leave some things unsaid and so I did. But I was as proud of this immigrant family as were her relatives gathered in this room.

After the picture taking we gathered around a table in the next room to eat the meal that the daughters-in-law had been scurrying to prepare. We began with a rich chicken soup, followed by pieces of beef in a thick sauce, lettuce, onions and cabbage, yogurt, fresh cheese and bread. Our taxi driver was with us every minute, clearly enjoying himself.

"I told him to wait in the car," whispered Esad, grinning, "but I guess that's not so much fun."

Later Hata's sister, Xhyla, suggested that we visit her home in the mountains that border Macedonia, and we eagerly assented. On the road south all the gas stations were new and the homes were either the burned out gutted remnants of the war or smart new brick homes constructed with western money that had poured in since the war. Hata's family had a lumber yard and the brisk business they had been doing was beginning to slow down, as the NGO's and foreign government agencies began to pack up and go home.

We drove, in Besniku's little VW, following his sister's large van, through the large town of Vitina, where she worked as a doctor at a clinic weekdays. Her husband Adem joined us for the trip up the mountain to his family's home.

The town was full of uniformed soldiers – the numerous Serbs who live in this area were at risk – and on the square a lone American soldier stood, his back to the greenery, eyes on the sidewalk crowds and finger on the trigger of his machine gun. He looked scared.

"We are in the American sector," Esad told us and as we looked around we saw the little icon of red, white and blue stars and stripes adorning jeeps and trucks and uniforms that otherwise looked like ones we had seen everywhere. There was a road block of barbed wire at the edge of town, manned by Americans. Our two cars edged slowly forward in the line and as we approached the two tall giants who were checking through the cars I stuck my head out the window and shouted in my best Midwestern accent.

"Hey, where ya' from?"

One soldier turned, spit a huge wad into the dust far from the car and moved up close to peer in the window.

"American?"

"Yeah."

"Where from?"

"Chicago!"

"Hey! I'm from Detroit."

The guy had been in the special forces 12 years. There was no fear in his face and his fingers hung loose, far from the trigger of his rifle. He waved us through.

We began the slow torturous climb up a route that seemed to be more river bed than road, maneuvering the ruts and rocks as the little engine worked and smoked and stunk.

"Tell Fidan to send his uncle a new car," Besniku said.

We reached a settlement, the tiny village of Buzovik, surrounded by herds of sheep. A huge UCK sign adorned a crumbling concrete wall and we passed through another road block.

"It was not like this yesterday." Besniku said, "Something is happening."

A lot was happening, but on the other side of the mountains. Albanians, who were as large a minority in Macedonia as they were in Montenegro and of course in Kosovo, were causing trouble for the government – the kind of trouble people cause when they get tired of being treated as second class citizens – and were being harassed by the Macedonian military. Afraid of another Kosovo, the country people were crossing the border back north through these Timrishave Mountains. Roadblocks were frequently set up at night, Besniku told us, but this was the first time they had appeared during the day, portending that things must be heating up in that country 3.6 miles beyond. There had been American bases on this border for six years, to keep the peace first between Macedonians and Serbians and now between Macedonians and Kosovars.

At Xhyla's home we were invited into the living room where we arranged ourselves in the traditional circle, drinking gritty Kosovar coffee. Esad was kept busy with the conversation as Mary and I were plied with questions. This extended family of Hata's brother-in-law were curious about her and her family in America, but in a less friendly fashion than had her own family been. I sensed a disapproval – perhaps an envy, perhaps something else – of the emigrating family. The patriarchal father-in-law sat stiffly in his white hat, younger people whom I gathered to be sons and daughters-in-law gathered around, and the head man of the Macedonian refugees, in his black hat, joined us for coffee. The mother-in-law wore baggy trousers, blouse, sweater and scarf tied in the back of the neck, exactly as her own mother probably had.

Later we walked down the hill to where 22 Macedonian refugees were sheltered in one of the houses on the large property. Children played outside, watched by young women who stood in groups and didn't smile as we passed. A young boy – surely no more than 12 – followed us, a cigarette drooping from the corner of his hard little mouth. It was a sylvan setting, a number of old but well-kept buildings surrounded by cows, horses and sheep, but it was also a war zone.

In the late afternoon we left and then, returning to Hata's home, we left again. Her stoic father's eyes were filled with tears as he said goodbye.

Our next adventure, the following day, was to find Henkelinda's roots. We rented a monstrous Nissan Terrano, a 4by4 diesel with high clearance, from a firm called Global Development Four LTD, located in the midst of a crow rookery outside the city. With me apprehensively at the wheel we were heading for Deçan when we pulled up behind a line of stopped cars that stretched across the valley below. The traffic was on its way to a special ceremony and the local police seemed unable to route the through traffic around. Finally, when the Italian KFOR truck in front of us, equipped with a team of gunners and guns on its trailer, pulled out into the opposite lane and sped off against the traffic, I followed close behind, with Esad screaming insults at the local police through the open window as we tore through town.

Henkelinda had told me only that her uncle ran a restaurant in Deçan and that everyone knew him. But the town was jammed with many restaurants and when we finally found the right one, he was not there. Esad persuaded one of the workers to climb into our car and he took us to the home of the famous Mehmet, Henkelinda's mother's brother. Famous at least to me, from Hita's song, as a dragon in the woods.

Creeping down a long and treacherous lane we finally ground to a halt and got out to walk. The house at the end was large and torn apart – pieces of the roof and walls were missing and we maneuvered a plank of wood to get beyond the rubble to the door where Mehmet, handsome and formal, came out to greet us as warmly as had everyone we'd met. We gathered on the ubiquitous circular sofas and were offered orange juice and coffee, while Mehmet's extended family gathered around. The room we were in had been finished, perfectly plastered and painted, but the rest of the house was a shambles. We were told that people couldn't get tiles for roofs and resorted to plastic as a cover. No one had money because they had no work. A nearby former furniture factory had never been reopened and a local resort hotel that had employed 200-300 people was closed, currently being used as a refugee camp. He said the IRC was working in Peć (Pea) and Jakova (Dakovica); but there was no capital investment coming in.

Mehmet was president of the local LDK in Deçan; he had been on the border and then in Albania during the NATO bombing. It was this house that his and Dyke's father had refused to leave, whose body was found after the Serbians left. Thanks to Hita, I was in awe of this man.

We followed him to lower Strelc to see the house where Henkelinda's family had lived, a large brick shell with pane-less windows and weeds growing in the center of the broken walls. We passed a Swedish electric company laying electric wire down the long bumpy road. It would provide the first electricity since the war.

Mary, Esad and Mehmet walking toward Henkelinda's former house

Later we continued north, along soaring snow-capped mountains to our west. Storms racing down from the mountains had created huge potholes, and brown streams of water poured over the pavement. The road was hell. Driving took all my skill, or lack of it. Mary's only comment later on my driving, which I did not appreciate, was that she would have made many different choices herself.

Yet we easily found Skenderaj, Hata and Xhela's hometown, with the aid of one of the few road signs we had seen. There was a second road sign, to the Jasari compound museum, where the massacre described by Xhela had occurred, but we did not follow it.

Just outside of town, to my chagrin, a policeman pulled me over for speeding, but confounded by my monologue in English, while the bilingual Esad appeared to be napping at my side, the policeman gave up in disgust and waved me on. The rain was now coming down in torrents but through the flapping window wipers we identified the hospital where Luan, Alban and Fidan had been born and peered up at the building where the Mehmeti apartment had been. I tried to make a connection between this house, this town, this street, and the horror stories Hata had told, but in vain. The rain, the policeman and the spectacular vistas across the countryside ran interference.

Esad had invited us to meet his mother and so, the following day, we took the same car to Belgiyzare, near Mitrovica. With her we walked up into the hills behind the little frame house as she told the story of escaping into those hills and only coming back to the house to cook bread at night. Afternoons they would watch the NATO planes roaring out of the sky, the bombs hitting in the valley. She, her three sons and daughter, lived three months in the woods, March-June 16th 1999. She remembered June 8th as the worst day, when 700 were taken prisoner and 16 killed.

One day, when she had come down with her daughter, Besarta, to bake bread, a Serbian soldier and a gypsy came to her house. The gypsy kept threatening to kill her, demanding . . .where is Madeline Albright's money?, where are Bill Clinton's bullets?

As we climbed high along the mountain path, she pointed to brown pools of water from which they drank, a pail, pieces of clothing, a child's sweater, part of a mattress, plastic sheeting, all remnants from their living in the woods. Her husband was with them at the beginning, and then he left. Her son, Ardina. went one day to another village for flour, and when he didn't come back for hours, she was terrified. When he finally arrived back in the camp there was a bullet hole through the sack of flour – one of the stories she told as we climbed about the now-peaceful wooded hills.

I asked Esad why his father had left his wife and children when there was such danger.

"To fight?" I asked.

"For another woman," he replied, "like Henkelinda's father."

I was astonished that he had known.

"Kosovar men are like that," added Esad. "It's why I'll never get married. I don't want to turn bad like my father did."

Esad saw himself as head of the family and talked about taking them to Canada. Yet with all his good spirits and warm heart, he was full of contradictions. He talked forgiveness, peace and reconciliation but wanted revenge against the Serbs; we had also seen his zest for wielding authority, his angry passions, but we allowed him anything. Mary and I were crazy about this guy.

Before we left we drove to the Ibar River, wanting to cross into Mitrovica. Hata and Xhela had once lived there and still owned a house in that town. We were stopped at the river's edge by a French member of KFOR… "too dangerous," he said. In northernmost Kosovo, Mitrovica was a largely Serbian town.

Back in Pristina, as our time was running out, we visited the University. When Henkelinda came home I had hoped she could attend. We talked with the Rector who told us there were 20,000 in the university, that it was overflowing with kids who couldn't find work and wanted to study, many having come back from Germany where they had been refugees. There were student accommodations but they were overcrowded. First come, first served, but very few were being served at all. I was beginning to think that there might not be much here for Henkelinda, when she returned.

One morning Rimsia appeared as we sat finishing our breakfast toast and jam. We had no idea what she had come for, since she spoke no English, but we left the restaurant and dragged a boy from behind the reception desk to interpret, which he did loudly and with interest in the content, while all the men lounging in the nearby deep leather lobby chairs inclined their heads our way. I have no recollection of what he and presumably she said; I guessed it was an incoherent plea for help.

On our last day in the country, Hamide invited the two of us on an excursion into the country – she had a family to meet with. At one point, totally lost, having bumped up and down winding and circular (as it turned out) roads, we stopped to ask. A group of men gathered around Hamide, all with different answers to her questions, refusing to take her seriously, obviously knowing no more than she did herself. But they had spotted Mary and me as Americans.

"Give me papers to visit America and I'll tell you where they live," one guy smirked. We gave up.

That afternoon she took us to see another family. We were ushered into a living room where five women – all widows – crowded around. They served coffee and juice drink and began to talk. Three of the older women (another was in a nearby bedroom, no longer rational) had lost three sons each. They were massacred in their own courtyard in February 1998.

My stomach began to churn. This was the Ahmeti family, the family Xhela had told me about, the one he went to visit, seeing human brains and teeth as he walked across the field. This old woman or more likely the one in the bedroom behind us, was she to whom he had paid respects, whose grandson had been returned to her in a body bag. I was completely paralyzed to think that we were in that place, among the women who had lost all of their men. I had no idea how to handle this thing and hoped that we would leave soon.

But one of the younger women pulled out a photo album and settled on the sofa between us two American women. Through the course of the long and agonizing afternoon she moved slowly from page to page, Mary asking questions about each male face she saw. To me it felt sadistic, this freshening of such painful memories, laying out for us the lost lives that they once had with young, middle aged and old men, all of whom were swept away in a single afternoon. Later, however, I understood what Mary had known all along, that it helped these women to move beyond their memories by exposing them to the light of day. It was our – at least Mary's – way of witnessing, of being truly present. Moving beyond this war would be a slow, excruciating process, for these Ahmeti women, for Hata's and Henkelinda's families, for Kosovo itself.

CHAPTER 13

HOW IT ALL TURNED OUT

It seems so long ago. Technology has erased the distance between Henkelinda and me and our occasional Skype conversations keep me up to date. She still lives in Germany, with her husband Izmet and their three sons. Her mother and the younger children live nearby, but across the border in Belgium. They have visited Kosovo but have successfully eluded the system that would return them; now they will never have to go back. Hita, Donika, Nimi and Gufim have reaped full benefits from the German schools, where they have all pursued paths into higher education. I do not know – nor ask – where Ali is. I expect to see them all again sometime. Perhaps in the United States.

Esad and his new family

I lost touch with Esad after our trip to Kosovo but to my amazement, I found him on Facebook and discovered that this boy who swore he would not marry now has a lovely wife and two daughters. Even more surprising, my granddaughter Stephanie saw his face on my screen saver, one day, and said "I know that man." They had played some silly internet game together. Stephanie also has had some internet contact with Donika who, along with Hita, are unrecognizable on their Facebook pages. How could those shy little refugee girls have blossomed into such spectacular young women?!

I stay in touch with Mary, and she stays in touch with Women for Women, in Sarajevo, Zagreb and Pristina. We have taken no more trips together, for which Dick would be grateful, had he not succumbed to cancer between then and now.

To my astonishment, as this book was going to press in the spring of 2014, Radislav Krstić was in the news again. He had been convicted in 2001 – the first person convicted of genocide at the ICTY – and sentenced to 35 years imprisonment. He had been assaulted by three Muslim inmates where he was being held in Wakefield Prison in northern England, and had just been removed to a specially guarded prison in Piotrkov Trybunalski in central Poland. Since Poland's maximum prison term is 25, the Polish courts will have to decide how much longer he should serve in his new one-person cell.

The international court at The Hague had, not surprisingly, proceeded in its careful, plodding way, to initiate proceedings against the other major players in the wars of former Yugoslavia. Slobodan Milosevic's trial began in 2002 but was terminated when he died in March, 2006. Ratko Mladić was extradited to The Hague in May 2011 and charged with two counts of genocide and other crimes against humanity. His trial began in May, 2012, the Prosecution case rested in February of 2014 and the Defense was scheduled to begin in May. Radovan Karadzic, another major Serbian player, was arrested in 2008, charged with genocide and other crimes against humanity, and his trial began in 2009. Closing arguments are scheduled for the fall of 2014. The wheels of justice may turn slowly, but they turn.

In Croatia, the goat that Milan bought and carried to Mirka in the trunk of his car turned out to be pregnant – a two-for-one!

* * *

It is more than a decade later and I am coming home from lunch with Hata. We get together, just the two of us, as often as we can. Sometimes I have dinner with them in their comfortable split level house in town; less often they troop out to the farm where they used to and I still live.

Hata talked at lunch about her family, her boys, and the lives they have made for themselves in their new country. As, one by one, each family member became a United States citizen, we remaining members of The Group trouped to their ceremonies, scattered across the Midwestern region of the federal Immigration Bureaucracy. The boys have become true Americans, which their parents will never be willing or able to be.

The Mehmetis at home in Michigan City. Luan, Xhela, Hata and Alban.

Alban, the middle son, having graduated from the University of Indiana, lives in Chicago where he works as a well-paid computer consultant and enjoys a lively bachelorhood. Luan, the youngest, graduated from Northwestern University this year, where he excelled academically, and is on his way to being an investment banker. Both he and Alban benefited from participation in the Evans Scholarship program, thanks to my son-in-law, Mike Merucci, who was himself a part of it many years ago.

The oldest son, Fidan, has taken a different route. He lives in an adjoining town with his wife, Arieta, and their two adorable sons, Edmund and Eliot.

I turn into the driveway and drive past the little farm house, available now for visits from children and grandchildren. The dog that greets me is not Bête Noire. Bête stretched out for a nap in the sunshine, many years ago, and never woke up. Wanting this dog to escape the specialness of Bête, I picked out a shorthaired male mutt at the pound, said to be part pit bull, and named him Scotty. That should make him so ordinary that he will never compete with Bête, I thought, but it was not to be. Carrying his own specialness in a different guise, his place in my heart is every bit as large as was Bête's.

I will watch the PBS News Hour tonight, my substitute for being on the front lines, wherever they may be. I see the world through Margaret's eyes and Gwen's questions might well be my own. My Friday evening chats with Mark and David exceed in interest and intelligence, by far, any three dimensional conversations I might have outside the darkened room. Thus I imagine myself to be connected to the greater world, although I am not.

Back then I was. From that serendipitous meeting with my Henkelinda at the Coca Cola refugee camp, I became truly present in the lives of her and Hata's families. It felt, and feels, quite good.

ACRONYMS USED IN THE BOOK

ICTY   International Criminal Tribunal for Yugoslavia
IRC   International Rescue Committee
KFOR   Kosovo stabilization force, a NATO operation
KLA   Kosovo Liberation Army
KVM   Kosovar Verification Mission
LDK   Democratic League of Kosovo
NATO   North Atlantic Treaty Organization
NGO   Non-governmental Organizations
OSCE   Organization for Security and Cooperation in Europe
RS   Serb Republika
SFOR   Sarajevo stabilization force, a NATO operation
UNHCR   United Nations High Commission on Refugees
UNICEF   The United Nations Children's Fund
VRS   The Serbian army
WHO   World Health Organization

BOOK CREDITS

Books that were drawn upon

- ➤ Balkan Ghosts, a Journey Through History. Robert Kaplan. Vintage Books, New York, 1993.
- ➤ Harvest in the Snow: My Crusade to Rescue the Lost Children of Bosnia, Ellen Blackman. Brassey's Inc., Washington, 1997.
- ➤ End Game: The Betrayal and Fall of Srebrenica: Europe's Worst Massacre Since World War II, David Rohde. Farrar Straus & Giroux, New York, 1997.
- ➤ Waging Modern War. General Wesley K. Clark. Public Affairs, New York, 2001.

41012625R00086

Made in the USA
San Bernardino, CA
02 November 2016